A–Z

of

Embroidered
Flowers

SEARCH PRESS

What greater delight is there than to behold the earth apparelled with plants, as with a robe of embroidered work.

from *The Herball* by John Gerard, published 1597

Lovers of embroidery are lovers of all things beautiful and the beauty of nature is captured most exquisitely in the glorious blooms nature throws at us each season.

It seems that so often a love of gardening and embroidering go hand in hand. This book is a celebration of both flowers and embroidery.

The following pages hold one hundred beautiful floral embroideries from familiar cottage garden plants to spring bulbs and Australian natives. They cover a wide variety of embroidery techniques from traditional surface embroidery to crewel embroidery, shadow work, wool and ribbon embroidery, thread painting and stumpwork. Use them to decorate your garments, your home, your life.

Warmest regards,

Sue Gardner, Editor

Contents

ALYSSUM

Alyssum maritimun by Carol Hawkins

Order of work

Use the photograph as a guide to thread colour changes within the design.

Foliage

Beginning at the base, work the main stems in encroaching stem stitch, gradually tapering into stem stitch for the upper sections. Add the leaves in satin or encroaching stem stitch and then the flower and bud stems in stem, back or straight stitch.

Flowers

Embroider each green bud with either a granitos of 2–3 straight stitches, a French knot or a detached chain.

Stitch each petal with either a granitos of 2–3 straight stitches or a detached chain. In the centre of each flower, work 1–2 very tiny straight stitches with the avocado green thread and then place a yellow French knot over the top.

This design uses

Back stitch, Detached chain,
Encroaching stem stitch,
French knot, Granitos, Satin stitch,
Stem stitch, Straight stitch

Requirements

Threads

Gumnut Yarns 'Stars' stranded silk
A = 549 dk forest green
B = 589 dk apple green
C = 708 dk lemon crush
Madeira stranded silk
D = 1407 avocado green
Au Ver à Soie, Soie d'Alger
E = blanc

Needle

No. 10 sharp needle

I've always thought my flowers
had souls.   *Myrtle Reed*

Embroidery key

All embroidery is worked with one strand of thread.

Flowers

Petals = E (detached chain, granitos)

Centres = C (French knot, 1 wrap), D (straight stitch)

Buds = A or B (detached chain, granitos, French knot, 1 wrap)

Foliage

Main stems = A or B (encroaching stem stitch, stem stitch)

Flower stems = A or B (stem stitch, straight stitch)

Bud stems = A or B (back stitch, stem stitch, straight stitch)

Leaves = A or B (encroaching stem stitch, satin stitch)

ANEMONES

Anemone coronia by Joan Gibson

This design uses
Detached chain, French knot, Stem stitch

Requirements

Threads

DMC stranded cotton
A = blanc
B = 209 lavender
C = 309 deep rose
D = 310 black
E = 333 vy dk blue-violet
F = 522 fern green
G = 3731 vy dk dusky rose

Needles
No. 7 crewel needle
No. 9 crewel needle

Order of work
Use the no. 7 crewel needle for the white French knots and the no. 9 crewel needle for all other embroidery.

Work a white French knot for the centre of each anemone. Beginning close to the centre, work stem stitch, spiralling outwards in tightly packed circles, until the flower is the desired size. Repeat for the remaining flowers, using the photograph as a guide to thread colour. Add a black French knot over the white one to complete each centre.

Embroider the stems in stem stitch and add the detached chain leaves.

Embroidery key

All embroidery is worked with two strands of thread unless otherwise specified.

Flowers

Petals = B, C, E or G (stem stitch)

Centre = A (4 strands, French knot, 1 wrap), D (1 strand, French knot, 1 wrap)

Stems = F (1 strand, stem stitch)

Leaves = F (detached chain)

---

by Di Kirchner

This design uses
Detached chain, French knot, Straight stitch

Requirements

Threads

DMC stranded cotton
A = blanc
B = 310 black
C = 327 vy dk lavender
D = 601 dk cranberry
E = 666 bright Christmas red
F = 3348 lt yellow-green

Needle
No. 9 crewel needle

Order of work
To begin the petals, work four radiating detached chains which divide the space into quarters. Stitch two detached chains in each quarter space. Add 6–7 tiny white straight stitches over the petals for markings.

Ensure the stitches fan out from the centre. Embroider tight clusters of three French knots for the centres.

Work a single long straight stitch for each stem and add two detached chains for the leaves.

Embroidery key

All embroidery is worked with two strands of thread unless otherwise specified.

Flowers

Petals = C, D or E (detached chain)

Petal markings = A (1 strand, straight stitch)

Centre = B (French knot, 1 wrap)

Stems = F (straight stitch)

Leaves = F (detached chain)

AQUILEGIA

Aquilegia vulgaris by Carol Hawkins

This design uses
French knot, Long and short stitch,
Satin stitch, Stem stitch, Straight stitch

Flowers worthy of paradise.   *John Milton*

Requirements

Threads

Gumnut Yarns 'Stars' stranded silk
A = 549 dk forest green
Madeira stranded silk
B = 0112 custard
C = 0503 baby pink
D = 0811 vy dk shell pink
E = 0812 dk shell pink
F = 0813 shell pink
G = 0815 vy lt shell pink
H = 2207 vy lt old gold
I = 2208 lt old gold
J = 2209 med old gold

Needle

No. 10 sharp needle

Order of work

Flowers

Using the photograph as a guide to thread colour, stitch the inner petals and then the outer petals in long and short stitch. Complete the petals of one flower before beginning those of the next. Add the petal markings to the two lower flowers.

Work a fan shape of straight stitches of varying lengths for the stamens of the left and upper flowers. Add French knots to the tips of the straight stitches. Beginning near the centre each time, work radiating straight stitches for the stamens of the flower on the right. Add French knots to the tips of the stitches.

Foliage

Embroider the leaves, leaf stems and bud using the lighter sections of the green thread. Stitch the flower stems, small leaves and bud calyx with the darker sections of the same thread.

Aquilegias are also known as columbines or granny's bonnets and have been known to gardeners and artists since at least medieval times.

Embroidery key

All embroidery is worked with one strand of thread.

Upper flower
Inner petals = B, F and G (long and short stitch)
Outer petals = D and E (long and short stitch)
Stamens = I (straight stitch, French knot, 2 wraps)

Flower on left
Petal markings = E (straight stitch)
Inner petals = F and G (long and short stitch)
Outer petals = D and E (long and short stitch)
Stamens = I (straight stitch), J (French knot, 2 wraps)

Flower on right
Inner petals = B and H (long and short stitch)
Outer petals = C and F (long and short stitch)
Petal markings = E (straight stitch)
Stamens = I (straight stitch, French knot, 2 wraps)

Bud
Petals = A (satin stitch)
Calyx = A (straight stitch)

Foliage
Stems = A (stem stitch)
Large leaves = A (long and short stitch)
Small leaves = A (straight stitch)

AZALEA

Azalea species by Di Kirchner

This design uses

Detached chain, Straight stitch

Requirements

Threads

DMC stranded cotton
A = 319 dk pistachio green
B = 603 cranberry
C = 605 vy lt cranberry
D = 743 yellow
E = 745 vy lt yellow

Needle

No. 9 crewel needle

Order of work

Embroider five detached chains for the petals of each flower. Using the darker shade, place a straight stitch within each detached chain.

Work groups of 2–3 leaves around the flowers, stitching them in the same manner as the petals.

Deciduous and evergreen azaleas

Commonly known to gardeners as azaleas, these small to medium leafed shrubs belong to the botanical section *Azalea* within the *Rhododendron* genus.

Flowers come in a variety of shapes and are borne in a profusion of small to large trusses.

Embroidery key

All embroidery is worked with one strand of thread unless otherwise specified.

Flower

Pink petals = C (2 strands, detached chain), B (straight stitch)

Yellow petals = E (2 strands, detached chain), D (straight stitch)

Leaves = A (detached chain, straight stitch)

Flowers of all heavens, and lovelier than their names.   *Lord Tennyson*

BLACK-EYED SUSAN

Rudbeckia hirta by Di Kirchner

This design uses

Detached chain, French knot,
Stem stitch

Requirements

Threads

DMC stranded cotton
A = 523 lt fern green
B = 742 lt tangerine
C = 745 vy lt yellow
D = 3021 vy dk Jacobean green

Needle

No. 9 crewel needle

Embroidery key

*All embroidery is worked with two strands
of thread unless otherwise specified.*

Flowers

Petals = B (detached chain)

Petal outlines = C (detached chain)

Inner centre = C (French knot, 1 wrap)

Outer centre = D (1 strand, French knot,
1 wrap)

Stems = A (stem stitch)

Leaves = A (stem stitch)

Order of work

Stitch the petals first. Using the tangerine thread, work four radiating detached chains which divide the space into quarters. Stitch two detached chains in each of the quarter spaces. Surround each petal with a detached chain in the lighter yellow thread. Embroider a tight cluster of yellow French knots in the centre. Encircle the yellow knots with tiny French knots using the Jacobean green thread. Stitch the remaining two flowers in the same manner.

Embroider each stem and leaf with stem stitch.

There are several flowers that claim the common name 'Black-eyed Susan'

Gazania splendens – showy South African blooms that are unsurpassed for summer colour and easy to grow.

Rudbeckia hirta – hardy daisies from the United States with raised centres of purple black.

Tetratheca ericifolia – miniature Australian native with masses of showy pink bells.

Thunbengia alata – climbing vine from South Africa with black-eyed, bright orange flowers.

The loveliest flowers the closest
cling to earth.   *John Keble*

BLUEBELL

Endymion non-scripta by Joan Gibson

This design uses
Bullion knot, Couching, French knot,
Stem stitch, Straight stitch

Requirements

Threads
DMC stranded cotton
A = 320 med pistachio green
B = 809 delft

Needles
No. 9 crewel needle
No. 9 straw (milliner's) needle

Order of work

Use the crewel needle for the stems
and leaves and the straw needle for
the flowers and buds.

Foliage
Work the stems in stem stitch.
Embroider each leaf with two
straight stitches, which use the same
holes in the fabric.

Flowers
Stitch the flowers and buds following
the step-by-step instructions below.

Embroidery key

*All embroidery is worked with one strand
of thread.*

Flowers

Upper flowers = B (2 bullion knots,
11 wraps, couching, straight stitch)

Lower flowers = B (2 bullion knots,
12–13 wraps, couching, straight stitch)

Buds = B (French knot, 1–2 wraps)

Foliage

Stems = A (stem stitch)

Leaves = A (straight stitch)

STEP-BY-STEP BLUEBELL

We used two strands of thread for photographic purposes.

† indicates top of fabric

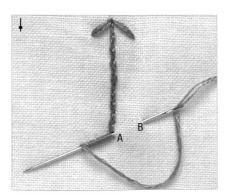

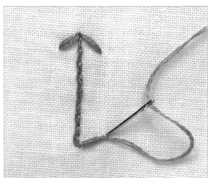

1 **Foliage.** Work the stem in stem stitch. Stitch two straight stitches, which use the same holes in the fabric, on each side of the stem.

2 **Flowers.** Turn the fabric upside down. Bring the thread to the front at A and take the needle from B to A. Wrap the thread around the needle eleven times.

3 Pull the thread through until the knot is thin and even. Take the needle to the back of the fabric.

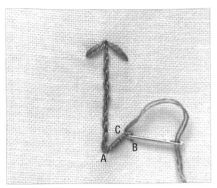

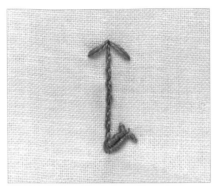

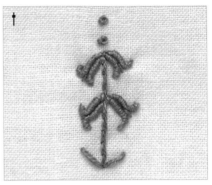

4 Pull the thread through. Re-emerge at C and couch the knot in place.

5 Stitch a second bullion knot as a mirror image of the first. If a gap exists between the knots, fill it with a straight stitch.

6 Work the remaining flowers in the same manner. Add two French knot buds at the top, using two wraps for the lower knot and one wrap for the upper knot.

BLUEBELL

Endymion non-scripta by Di Kirchner

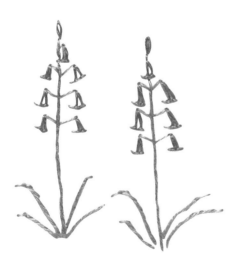

This design uses
Blanket stitch, Detached chain, Stem stitch, Straight stitch

Requirements

Threads
DMC stranded cotton
A = 368 lt pistachio green
B = 794 lt cornflower blue

Needle
No. 9 crewel needle

Order of work

Embroider the main stems and leaves in stem stitch. On each plant, stitch seven flowers using two blanket stitches to create each one. Add a detached chain bud directly above the top flower.

Connect each flower to the main stem with a straight stitch.

Bluebells – constancy.
The Language of Flowers

Embroidery key

All embroidery is worked with one strand of thread.

Flowers
Petals = B (blanket stitch)
Buds = B (detached chain)

Foliage
Main stems = A (stem stitch)
Flower stems = A (straight stitch)
Leaves = A (stem stitch)

BOTTLEBRUSH

Callistemon citrinus by Joan Gibson

This design uses
Chain stitch, Fly stitch, French knot, Granitos, Stem stitch, Straight stitch

Embroidery key

All embroidery is worked with one strand of thread unless otherwise specified.

Open flower

Centre line = B (2 strands, chain stitch)

Stamens = A (straight stitch, French knot, 1 wrap)

Opening flower

Centre line = B (stem stitch)

Opening buds = B (fly stitch), A (straight stitch, French knot, 1 wrap)

Closed buds = B (granitos)

Foliage

Stems = B (stem stitch)

Large leaves = B (stem stitch)

Small leaves = B (straight stitch)

Requirements

Threads
DMC stranded cotton
A = 350 med coral
B = 3347 med yellow-green

Needle
No. 9 crewel needle

Order of work

Open flower
Stitch the green centre line in chain stitch. From the centre of every alternate chain stitch, work 4–5 straight stitches of varying lengths radiating out on each side. Add a French knot near the tip of each straight stitch.

Foliage
Embroider the stems in stem stitch, working the left hand stem up to the tip of the flower. Outline the six large leaves and fill them with rows of stem stitch packed closely together.

   Stitch five small leaves at the tip of the open flower and three at the tip of the stem for the opening flower. For each one, work 3–4 straight stitches, which share the same hole in the fabric at the tip.

Opening flower
Work 3–5 straight stitches for the stamens. Add French knots to the two lower groups.

   Work a fly stitch around the base of each group, except for the two towards the top.

   Below the small leaves, embroider four closed buds along the stem. Work a granitos of 3–4 straight stitches for each one.

BUDDLEIA

Buddleia davidii by Carol Hawkins

This design uses

Back stitch, Encroaching stem stitch, French knot, Granitos,
Long and short stitch, Satin stitch, Straight stitch

Requirements

Threads

DMC stranded cotton
A = 319 dk pistachio green
B = 320 med pistachio green
C = 433 med brown
D = 520 dk fern green
E = 522 fern green
F = 524 vy lt fern green
G = 718 med fuchsia
H = 721 med orange spice
I = 3607 fuchsia
J = 3608 lt fuchsia

Needle

No. 10 sharp needle

Order of work

Use the photograph as a guide
to thread colour changes within
the design.

Foliage

Stitch the main stem and then the two
secondary stems. Embroider all the
leaves in satin stitch. Work the leaf
veins and outlines. Stitch the flower
and bud stems next.

Flowers

Embroider tiny granitos of 2–3 straight
stitches for the petals of the flowers.
Add French knot centres to most of
the flowers. Work the buds using either
a French knot or 1–2 very small
straight stitches.

Embroidery key

All embroidery is worked with one strand of thread.

Flowers

Petals = G, I and J (granitos)

Centres = H (French knot, 1 wrap) or none

Buds = G, I and J (straight stitch, French knot,
1 wrap)

Stems

Main stem = C, E and F (encroaching
stem stitch, long and short stitch, satin stitch)

Secondary stems = F (satin stitch)

Flower stems = F (straight stitch, back stitch)

Bud stems = F (straight stitch)

Leaves

Large leaves = A and F (satin stitch)

Veins and outlines on large leaves = D
(back stitch) or none

Highlight to lower left leaf = B (satin stitch)

Small leaves = A, B, E and F (satin stitch)

Flowers are made to seduce the senses:
fragrance, form, colour.   *Hilda Doolittle*

BOUGAINVILLEA

Bougainvillea glabra by Di Kirchner

This design uses
Detached chain, French knot,
Straight stitch

Requirements

Threads
DMC stranded cotton
A = 746 off-white
B = 3347 med yellow-green
C = 3607 fuchsia

Needle
No. 9 crewel needle

Order of work

Embroider five detached chains for the
petals of each flower. Add a French
knot to the centre of each one. Scatter
tiny detached chain and straight stitch
leaves among the flowers.

Embroidery key

*All embroidery is worked with one strand
of thread.*

Flowers

Petals = C (detached chain)

Centres = A (French knot, 1 wrap)

Leaves = B (detached chain, straight stitch)

CAMELLIA

Camellia japonica by Di Kirchner

This design uses
Blanket stitch, Couching,
Detached chain, French knot,
Straight stitch

Requirements

Threads
DMC stranded cotton
A = 520 dk fern green
B = 602 med cranberry
C = 677 vy lt old gold
D = 783 med topaz

Needle
No. 9 crewel needle

Order of work

Flowers

Stitch the flowers following the
step-by-step instructions on page 15.
Work a fan shape of 2–3 blanket
stitches for the petals of the buds.

Foliage

Stitch the stems in straight stitch,
couching the longest stem. Embroider
detached chains for the leaves and
sepals of the buds.

Embroidery key

*All embroidery is worked with two strands
of thread unless otherwise specified.*

Flowers

Petals = B (blanket stitch)

Centres = C blended with D (1 strand of each,
French knot, 1 wrap)

Buds = B (blanket stitch)

Bud sepals = A (detached chain)

Stems = A (straight stitch, couching)

Leaves = A (detached chain)

STEP-BY-STEP CAMELLIA

We used contrasting thread for photographic purposes.

1 Petals. Trace the design onto the fabric. Bring the thread to the front on the outer line in the dip between two petals.

2 Work blanket stitches between the two marked design lines until reaching the starting point.

3 Take the needle to the back of the fabric just over the first stitch.

4 Pull the thread through. Re-emerge on the inner design line.

5 Stitch a second round of blanket stitch between the centre and the inner line. Begin each stitch from same hole in fabric. The 'purls' will just cover inner edge of previous round.

6 Centre. Using blended threads, work a cluster of five French knots.

There are over 250 different species of Camellias with more than 2,500 named varieties. *Camellia sasanqua* are first to flower in autumn, then the outstandingly varied *Camellia japonica* begin their main flush in winter, lasting well into late spring. The most spectacular of them all, *Camellia reticulata*, bloom in spring with flowers sometimes reaching almost 25cm (10") in width.

CARNATION

Dianthus caryophyllus by Di Kirchner

This design uses
Fly stitch, Straight stitch

Requirements

Threads

DMC stranded cotton
A = 335 rose
B = 353 peach
C = 504 vy lt blue-green
D = 963 ultra lt dusky rose

Needle
No. 9 crewel needle

Order of work

Flowers

To begin the petals of the first flower, work short straight stitches of varying lengths that radiate from the centre. Embroider a second row of straight stitches around the previous stitches.

Work the petals of the remaining flowers in the same manner.

Foliage

Starting directly below a flower, work a straight stitch approximately 2–3mm (⅛") long. Continuing with the same thread, stitch three fly stitches, one below the other.

CLOVER

Trifolium repens by Heather Scott

This design uses
Detached chain, Fly stitch, Stem stitch, Straight stitch

Requirements

Threads

DMC stranded cotton
A = blanc
B = 3347 med yellow-green
C = 3713 vy lt salmon

Needle
No. 10 sharp needle

Order of work

Both flowers are stitched in exactly the same manner. Beginning at the top of the flower, work the flower head with rows of white overlapping detached chains. Change to the pink thread. Continue working rows of overlapping detached chains to the base of the flower.

Beginning each leaf at the tip, embroider them in closely worked fly stitches with short anchoring stitches. Stitch the stems in stem stitch and sepals in stem and straight stitch.

CLIVIA

Clivia miniata by Di Kirchner

This design uses
Detached chain, French knot, Pistil stitch, Stem stitch, Straight stitch

Requirements

Threads
DMC stranded cotton
A = 350 med coral
B = 469 avocado green
C = 744 lt yellow

Needle
No. 9 sharp needle

Order of work

Flowers
Embroider six detached chains and place a straight stitch within each one to form the petals of each flower. Using a mix of straight and pistil stitches that fan out from the base, stitch the centres of the three larger flowers. Fill the centre of the smaller flower with four French knots.

Buds
Stitch three overlapping detached chains, each with a straight stitch inside them, for the petals. Work two detached chains that use the same hole in the fabric at the base of the bud for each sepal. Link the buds to the small flower with straight stitch stems.

Leaves
Work two rows of stem stitch, side by side, to form each leaf.

Embroidery key

All embroidery is worked with one strand of thread unless otherwise specified.

Flowers

Petals = A (2 strands, detached chain, straight stitch)

Centres of large flowers = C (pistil stitch, straight stitch)

Centre of small flower = C (French knot, 1 wrap)

Buds = A (2 strands, detached chain, straight stitch)

Bud sepals = B

(detached chain)

Stems and leaves

Bud stems = B (straight stitch)

Leaves = B (stem stitch)

CORNFLOWER

Centaurea cyanus by Joan Gibson

This design uses
Padded satin stitch, Stem stitch,
Straight stitch

Requirements

Threads

DMC stranded cotton
A = 310 black
B = 792 dk cornflower blue
C = 989 vy lt forest green

Needle

No. 9 crewel needle

Order of work

Foliage

Stitch the stems and large leaves first,
followed by each calyx. At the top of
each stem, work 3–5 horizontal straight
stitches for padding. Cover these with
a layer of vertical satin stitches.
Embroider two straight stitches that
use the same holes in the fabric for
each small leaf.

Facing flowers

To begin the petals, work four straight
stitches leaving a space in the centre
(*see diag., below*). Stitch three petals of
varying lengths in each quarter space.
Using the black thread, embroider 9–11
straight stitches over the blue petals
and in the spaces between. Take these
stitches slightly further into the centre
than the blue stitches.

Back view flower

Work petals of varying lengths and
angles from the top of the calyx.

Embroidery key

*All embroidery is worked with one strand
of thread unless otherwise specified.*

Flowers
Petals = B (2 strands, straight stitch)
Petal markings = A (straight stitch)
Calyxes = C (padded satin stitch)

Foliage
Stems = C (stem stitch)
Large leaves = C (stem stitch)
Small leaves = C (straight stitch)

CROCUS

Crocus corsicus by Di Kirchner

This design uses
Detached chain, Straight stitch

Requirements

Threads

DMC stranded cotton
A = 211 lt lavender
B = 3346 hunter green

Needle

No. 9 crewel needle

Order of work

Stitch the petals with three detached chains which all begin at the same position. Fan the stitches slightly.

Add straight stitches of varying lengths for the stems and leaves.

A farmer must harvest 4,320 crocus flowers to make one ounce of saffron.

Embroidery key

All embroidery is worked with two strands of thread.

Flowers = A (detached chain)

Stems and leaves = B (straight stitch)

CYCLAMEN

Cyclamen persicum by Joan Gibson

This design uses
Blanket stitch, Detached chain, Stem stitch

Requirements

Threads

DMC stranded cotton
A = 503 med blue-green
B = 899 med rose

Needle

No. 10 crewel needle

Order of work

Work the leaves in blanket stitch, radiating all the stitches from the same point. Add the stems in stem stitch.

At the tip of each stem, work two detached chains to form the flowers.

Embroidery key

All embroidery is worked with one strand of thread.

Flowers = B (detached chain)

Stems = A (stem stitch)

Leaves = A (blanket stitch)

DAFFODIL

Narcissus by Carolyn Pearce

This design uses

Blanket stitch, Detached buttonhole stitch, Fly stitch, French knot, Stem stitch, Straight stitch, Whipped chain stitch

Requirements

Threads

DMC stranded cotton
A = 921 copper
The Gentle Art sampler thread
B = avocado
YLI silk floss
C = 97 French beige
YLI no. 50 silk thread
D = 078 mustard

Needles

No. 10 crewel needle
No. 26 tapestry needle

Order of work

Use the tapestry needle for the detached buttonhole stitch and the crewel needle for all other embroidery.

Flowers

Each flower is stitched in the same manner. Embroider the trumpet first, beginning with a blanket stitch pinwheel. Roll the 'purls' towards the centre and change needles. Work one detached buttonhole stitch into each of the next two blanket stitches, then two detached buttonhole stitches into the next blanket stitch. Repeat this sequence until the round is complete. Stitch a second row, working one stitch into the top of each stitch of the previous row.

Work a French knot inside the trumpet for the centre. Stitch six petals on the facing daffodils and four on the side view daffodil. For each petal, work five straight stitches which share the same hole in the fabric at the tip but fan out at the base. Surround the straight stitches with a fly stitch.

Stems and leaves

Stitch the stems in whipped chain stitch. Work three rows of stem stitch, side by side, for each leaf.

I wandered lonely as a cloud
That floats on high o'er vales and hills,
When all at once I saw a crowd,
A host, of golden daffodils;
Beside the lake, beneath the trees,
Fluttering and dancing in the breeze

Continuous as the stars that shine
And twinkle on the milky way,
They stretched in never-ending line
Along the margin of a bay:
Ten thousand saw I at a glance,
Tossing their heads in sprightly dance.

William Wordsworth, 1770–1850

Embroidery key

All embroidery is worked with one strand of thread unless otherwise specified.

Flowers

Trumpets = D (blanket stitch, detached buttonhole stitch)

Petals = C (straight stitch, fly stitch)

Centres = A (2 strands, French knot, 1 wrap)

Stems = B (2 strands, whipped chain stitch)

Leaves = B (stem stitch)

DAFFODIL

Narcissus by Joan Gibson

This design uses

Blanket stitch, Detached chain, Stem stitch, Straight stitch

Requirements

Threads

DMC stranded cotton
A = 523 lt fern green
B = 743 yellow

Needle

No. 10 crewel needle

Order of work

Flowers

Embroider 2–4 blanket stitches in a fan shape to form the trumpets. Add 2–3 detached chains to the base of each trumpet for the petals.

Change to the green thread. Work three straight stitches over the base of the petals for each calyx.

Stems and leaves

Stitch the stems in stem stitch, curving them into the base of the clump. Again, using stem stitch, embroider the leaves.

Embroidery key

All embroidery is worked with one strand of thread.

Flowers

Trumpets = B (blanket stitch)
Petals = B (detached chain)
Calyxes = A (straight stitch)
Stems = A (stem stitch)
Leaves = A (stem stitch)

It is thought that the name Daffodil probably comes from Affodyle, an old English word meaning early-comer.
The Language of Flowers

DAFFODIL

Narcissus by Gerda O'Brien

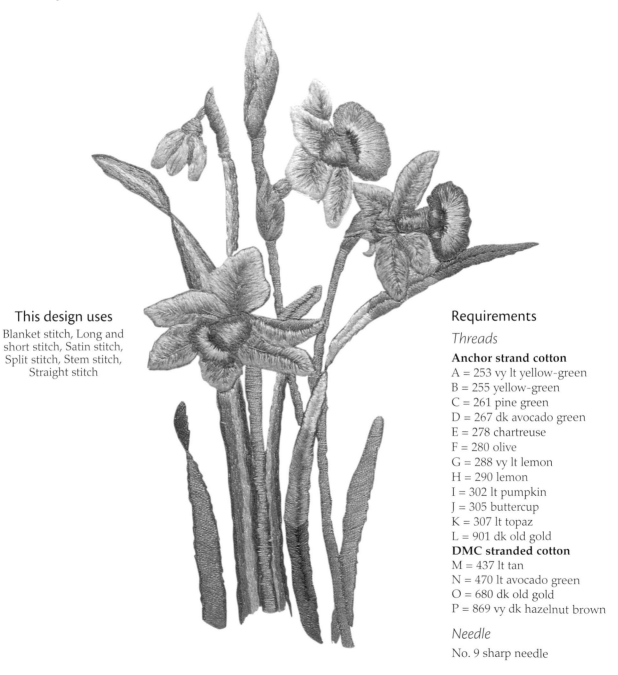

This design uses

Blanket stitch, Long and
short stitch, Satin stitch,
Split stitch, Stem stitch,
Straight stitch

Requirements

Threads

Anchor strand cotton
A = 253 vy lt yellow-green
B = 255 yellow-green
C = 261 pine green
D = 267 dk avocado green
E = 278 chartreuse
F = 280 olive
G = 288 vy lt lemon
H = 290 lemon
I = 302 lt pumpkin
J = 305 buttercup
K = 307 lt topaz
L = 901 dk old gold
DMC stranded cotton
M = 437 lt tan
N = 470 lt avocado green
O = 680 dk old gold
P = 869 vy dk hazelnut brown

Needle

No. 9 sharp needle

Order of work

Use the photograph as a guide to thread colour changes within the design.

Open flowers

Each open flower is worked in a similar manner. Embroider the trumpets first, working a row of blanket stitch around the frill and filling in the trumpet with long and short stitch. Add the highlights in straight stitch. Outline the back of two trumpets in split stitch.

Embroider the petals in long and short stitch. Stitch the curling petal of the lower daffodil in satin stitch.

Work straight stitches for highlights and outline the petals with stem stitch.

Changing thread colour, work the hoods of the two top daffodils in long and short stitch and satin stitch. Stitch each calyx in satin stitch.

Buds

Work the petals of the buds in long and short stitch. Outline the petals in split stitch. Work the hoods in a similar manner to those of the open flowers.

Stitch the calyx of the drooping bud in satin stitch.

Stems and leaves

Embroider the stems of the two upper flowers in satin stitch and the stem of the lower flower in long and short stitch. Work the stem of the drooping bud in long and short stitch and the partial stem of the upright bud in satin stitch.

Stitch the two shorter leaves and the curved leaf on the right in satin stitch. Outline the two shorted leaves in stem stitch and partially outline the curved leaf in the same manner. Work the tall leaf on the left in long and short stitch and the middle leaf in satin stitch.

Embroidery key

All embroidery is worked with two strands of thread unless otherwise specified.

Upper flower

Trumpet = K (blanket stitch) G, I, K and P (long and short stitch)

Trumpet highlights = F (1 strand, straight stitch)

Petals = G and I (long and short stitch)

Petal highlights = F and L (1 strand, straight stitch)

Petal outlines = G, L and O (1 strand, stem stitch, straight stitch) or none

Calyx = C (satin stitch), G and K (1 strand, straight stitch)

Hood = M and O (long and short stitch) C (1 strand, straight stitch)

Flower on left

Trumpet = L (blanket stitch), I, J, L and P (long and short stitch, straight stitch)

Trumpet highlights = G (1 strand, straight stitch)

Outline of trumpet back = L (1 strand, split stitch)

Petals = F (satin stitch), I, J and K (long and short stitch), J (1 strand, straight stitch)

Petal highlights = F (1 strand, straight stitch)

Petal outlines = K (stem stitch) or none

Flower on right

Trumpet = L (blanket stitch), G, I, L and P (long and short stitch), G and I (1 strand, straight stitch)

Trumpet highlights = F and H (1 strand, straight stitch)

Outline of trumpet back = L (1 strand, split stitch)

Calyx = C and D (satin stitch) D, G and K (1 strand, straight stitch)

Petals = H, I and K (long and short stitch, 1 strand, straight stitch)

Petal highlights = A, F and H (1 strand, straight stitch)

Petal outlines = K (1 strand, stem stitch) or none

Hood = M and O (long and short stitch, satin stitch), C (1 strand, straight stitch)

Drooping bud

Petals = G and I (long and short stitch)

Petal highlights = K (1 strand, straight stitch)

Petal outlines = F (1 strand, straight stitch) K (1 strand, straight stitch)

Calyx = C (satin stitch), G and K (1 strand, straight stitch)

Calyx outline = K (1 strand, straight stitch)

Hood = M and O (satin stitch)

Upright bud

Petals = C, G and I (long and short stitch)

Hood = M and O (satin stitch)

Stems

Flowers = A and B (long and short stitch), D (1 strand, split stitch), or C (satin stitch)

Drooping bud = A and B (long and short stitch), D (1 strand, stem stitch)

Upright bud = C (satin stitch)

Leaves

Short leaf on left = C (satin stitch, 1 strand stem stitch)

Tall leaf on left = A, B and D (long and short stitch, split stitch)

Centre leaf = N (satin stitch)

Tall leaf on right = A, B and D (satin stitch), D (1 strand, stem stitch) or none

Short leaf on right = N (satin stitch, 1 strand stem stitch)

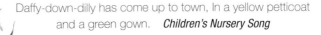

Daffy-down-dilly has come up to town, In a yellow petticoat and a green gown. *Children's Nursery Song*

DAHLIA

Dahlia variabilis by Di Kirchner

This design uses
Detached chain and French knot combination, French knot, Stem stitch, Straight stitch

Requirements

Threads

DMC stranded cotton
A = 744 lt yellow
B = 3347 med yellow-green

Needle
No. 9 sharp needle

Order of work

Each petal is a detached chain with a French knot worked for the anchoring stitch, rather than the usual tiny straight stitch. Beginning each petal near the centre, work a circle of petals. Overlay these with a second and third layer until the centre is filled and the flower is quite raised in the middle. Add a tiny French knot to the centre.

Stitch three petals in the same manner to form the bud.

Work the stems in stem stitch. Add detached chains for the leaves and place a straight stitch inside each one.

Embroidery key

All embroidery is worked with two strands of thread.

Flower

Petals = A (detached chain – French knot combination, 1 wrap)

Centre = A (French knot, 1 wrap)

Bud = A (detached chain – French knot combination, 1 wrap)

Stems = B (stem stitch)

Leaves = B (detached chain, straight stitch)

DAISY

Chrysanthemum frutescens by Judy Wearne

This design uses
Back stitch, French knot, Straight stitch

Requirements

Threads

DMC stranded cotton
A = blanc
B = 503 med blue-green
C = 745 vy lt yellow

Needle
No. 10 crewel needle

Order of work

Stitch the petals first, working two straight stitches that share the same hole in the fabric at the tip for each one. Work a round of petals, varying the lengths of the stitches. Work a second round of petals which lie between and on top of the first round. Fill the centre with tightly packed French knots. Embroider the stem and leaves in back stitch.

Embroidery key

All embroidery is worked with one strand of thread.

Flower

Petals = A (straight stitch)

Centre = C (French knot, 1 wrap)

Stem and leaves = B (back stitch)

DAISY

Leucanthemum x superbum by Di Kirchner

This design uses

Detached chain, Fly stitch, French knot, Stem stitch, Straight stitch

Requirements

Threads

DMC stranded cotton
A = blanc
B = 520 dk fern green
C = 744 lt yellow

Needle

No. 9 sharp needle

Order of work

Flowers

Stitch a circle of closely spaced detached chains for the petals of the facing flower and a half circle for the petals of the flower on the left. Work five detached chains in a fan shape for the petals of the bud. Add tight clusters of yellow French knots for the centres of the two flowers.

Foliage

Work the stems in stem stitch. Add three detached chains over the base of the bud for its calyx.

Embroider fly stitches with a straight stitch between the 'arms' of each fly stitch, for the leaves.

To create a little flower is the labour of ages. *William Blake*

Embroidery key

All embroidery is worked with two strands of thread.

Flowers

Petals = A (detached chain)

Centres = C (French knot, 1 wrap)

Bud

Petals = A (detached chain)

Calyx = B (detached chain)

Stems = B (stem stitch)

Leaves = B (fly stitch, straight stitch)

DAISIES

by Kris Richards

This design uses

Bullion knot, Bullion loop,
Detached chain, French knot,
Granitos, Straight stitch

Embroidery key

All embroidery is worked with two strands of thread unless otherwise specified.

Dark blue daisies

Petals = I (1 strand, bullion loop, 14 wraps)

Centres = H (French knot, 2 wraps)

Leaves = J (detached chain)

White daisies

Petals = A (straight stitch)

Centres = F (French knot, 2 wraps)

Leaves = L (detached chain)

Purple daisies

Petals = B and D (detached chain)

Centres = B (French knot, 2 wraps)

Leaves = C (detached chain)

Pale blue daisies

Petals = K (detached chain)

Centres = H (French knot, 2 wraps)

Leaves = J (detached chain)

Yellow daisies

Petals = H (1 strand, 2 bullion knots, 12 wraps)

Centres = G (French knot, 2 wraps)

Leaves = L (detached chain)

Pink daisies

Petals = E (granitos)

Centres = H (French knot, 2 wraps)

Leaves = C (detached chain)

Requirements

Threads

DMC stranded cotton

A = blanc
B = 208 dk lavender
C = 370 med verdigris
D = 554 lt violet
E = 605 vy lt cranberry
F = 729 med old gold
G = 743 yellow
H = 745 vy lt yellow
I = 794 lt cornflower blue
J = 3023 lt Jacobean green
K = 3747 vy lt blue-violet

Anchor stranded cotton

L = 842 vy lt khaki green

Needles

No. 9 straw (milliner's) needle
No. 9 crewel needle

Order of work

Use the straw needle when working the French knots, bullion knots and loops. Use the crewel needle for all other embroidery.

Dark blue daisies

Stitch five bullion loops for the petals of each flower. Add French knots for the centres and detached chains for the leaves.

White daisies

Work a circle of twelve straight stitches for the petals of each flower. Add the centres and leaves in the same manner as the dark blue daisies.

Purple daisies

Stitch a circle of twelve large detached chains. Place a small detached chain inside each one. Add French knot centres and detached chain leaves.

Pale blue daisies

Work 5–6 detached chain petals. Add the centres and leaves in the same manner as the dark blue daisies.

Yellow daisies

Stitch two bullion knots, side by side, for each petal. Add the centres and leaves in the same manner as before.

Pink daisies

Work a granitos of five straight stitches for each petal. Add the centres and leaves in the same manner as before.

DAISY

Leucanthemum x superbum by Helen Eriksson

This design uses

Couching, Fly stitch,
French knot,
Ribbon stitch,
Straight stitch, Twisting

Requirements

Threads & ribbons

Anchor stranded cotton
A = 310 vy dk topaz
B = 845 dk khaki green

YLI silk ribbon 4mm (³⁄₁₆″) wide
C = 3 white
D = 15 bright golden yellow
E = 34 pale honey
F = 52 dk old gold
G = 54 gold
H = 171 avocado green

Needles

No. 8 straw (milliner's) needle
No. 18 chenille needle
No. 22 chenille needle

Embroidery key

All thread embroidery is worked with one strand.

Flower

Petals = C and E (ribbon stitch)

Centre = D, F and G
(French knot, 1 wrap)

Centre outline = A (French knot,
1 wrap)

Buds

Petals = C and E (ribbon stitch)

Centre of largest bud = F and G
(French knot, 1 wrap)

Centre outline of largest bud = A
(French knot, 1 wrap)

Sepals = H (ribbon stitch)

Foliage

Stems = H (twisting),
B (couching)

Leaves = H
(ribbon stitch, twisting, fly stitch,
straight stitch)

Order of work

Use the no. 18 chenille needle for the petals and sepals, the no. 22 chenille needle for the remaining ribbon embroidery and the straw needle for all thread embroidery.

Flower

Using the white ribbon, embroider ribbon stitch petals around the oval shaped centre. To achieve a realistic look, leave gaps every now and then and make some petals slightly shorter than the others.

Change to the pale honey ribbon and add approximately twelve petals. Stitch these petals beneath the previous ones.

Beginning with the darkest ribbon, stitch French knots in the lower portion of the centre. Change to the medium shade and work the middle section. Use the lightest shade for the upper section. Outline the sides and lower edge of the centre with French knots in the topaz thread.

Buds

To stitch the petals of the two smaller buds, work four ribbon stitches in the white ribbon. Overlay the base of these stitches with 4–5 ribbon stitches in the pale honey ribbon. Leave approximately two thirds of the white petals showing.

Embroider five white petals for the back of the largest bud. Using the two gold ribbons, stitch the centre in a similar manner to the flower centre. Outline the upper edge with tiny French knots. Add five white ribbon stitches for the foremost petals.

Work 3–4 ribbon stitches for the sepals of each bud.

Foliage

Each stem is formed in the same manner. Bring the ribbon to the front at the top of a stem.

Twist the ribbon in a clockwise direction until it is completely twisted. Take the ribbon to the back at the lower end. Repeat for the remaining stems and then couch them in place with the green thread.

Using twisted ribbon, work the leaves in fly and straight stitches. Finally, add the small ribbon stitch leaves to the main stem.

ENGLISH DAISY

Bellis perennis by Joan Gibson

This design uses

Detached chain, Fly stitch, French knot, Satin stitch, Stem stitch, Straight stitch

Requirements

Threads

DMC stranded cotton
A = blanc
B = 320 med pistachio green
C = 347 vy dk salmon
D = 725 dk golden yellow

Needle

No. 9 crewel needle

Order of work

Begin the two mature daisies with four straight stitches, dividing each flower into quarters. Fill each quarter space with several more white straight stitches.

Embroider a tiny fly stitch at the tip of each straight stitch.

For the bud, work four straight stitches, fanning them slightly at the tips. Edge the tips with fly stitches in the same manner as the mature flowers.

Stitch the stems in stem stitch and the bud calyx in satin stitch. Beginning each stitch near the same position, embroider six large detached chains for the leaves.

I'd choose to be a daisy,
If I might be a flower. **Anonymous**

Embroidery key

All embroidery is worked with one strand of thread unless otherwise specified.

Flowers

Petals = A (2 strands, straight stitch)

Petal tips = C (fly stitch)

Centres = D (French knot, 1 wrap)

Bud calyx = B (satin stitch)

Stems = B (stem stitch)

Leaves = B (2 strands, detached chain)

FORGET-ME-NOT

Myosotis sylvatica by Carolyn Pearce

This design uses

Beading, Couching, Detached chain

Requirements

Threads & Beads

The Thread Gatherer Silk 'n Colors stranded silk
A = SNC 027 maidenhair fern
Maria George size 11 embroidery beads
B = 6130 beige
C = 6171 pastel blue

Needle

No. 10 straw (milliner's) needle

Supplies

Nymo beading thread

Order of work

Embroider the flowers following the step-by-step instructions on this page. Add two detached chain leaves with long anchoring stitches alongside each forget-me-not.

Embroidery key

All thread embroidery is worked with one strand.

Flowers
Petals = C
(beading, couching)
Centres = B (beading)

Leaves = A
(detached chain)

STEP-BY-STEP BEADED FORGET-ME-NOT

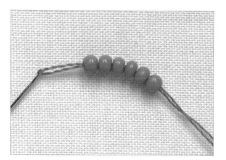

1 **Flower.** Using a 30cm (12") length of *Nymo* thread and the straw needle, thread on six blue beads.

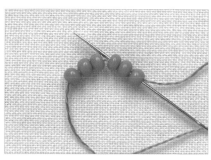

2 Pass the needle and thread through the first three beads to form a circle.

3 Thread on a beige bead. Take the needle and thread through the sixth blue bead.

4 Pull firmly so the centre bead sits in the middle, slightly higher than the circle of blue beads.

5 Tightly knot the two ends of thread. Use one of the tails to couch the circle of beads to the fabric.

6 Take the ends to the back and end off. **Leaves.** Work detached chain leaves using long anchoring stitches.

FORGET-ME-NOT

Myosotis sylvatica by Carolyn Pearce

This design uses
Beading, Colonial knot, Detached chain

Requirements

Threads & Beads
DMC stranded cotton
A = 3840 lt lavender blue
The Thread Gatherer Silk 'n Colors stranded silk
B = SNC 027 maidenhair fern
Mill Hill glass seed beads
C = 00557 gold

Needles
No. 7 crewel needle
No. 10 crewel needle

Supplies
Nymo beading thread

Order of work

Use the no. 7 crewel needle for the flower petals and the no. 10 crewel needle for the leaves and attaching the beads.

Attach a single bead for the centre of each flower. Stitch the colonial knot petals in the order shown on the diagram *(see diag., above right)*. Bring the thread to the front a tiny distance from the bead, work the knot and anchor it by taking the needle and thread to the back under the bead. Repeat for the remaining petals.

Add pairs of detached chains with long anchoring stitches between the flowers for the leaves.

Embroidery key
All embroidery is worked with one strand of thread unless otherwise specified.
Flowers
Petals = A (4 strands, colonial knot)
Centres = C (beading)
Leaves = B (detached chain)

FORGET-ME-NOT

Myosotis sylvatica by Carolyn Pearce

This design uses

Colonial knot, Detached chain,
Fly stitch, French knot, Granitos,
Stem stitch

Requirements

Threads

DMC stranded cotton
A = 778 vy lt antique mauve
B = 3841 pale baby blue
YLI silk floss
C = 181 pale caramel
**The Thread Gatherer Silk 'n Colors
stranded silk**
D = SNC 027 maidenhair fern

Needles

No. 5 crewel needle
No. 10 crewel needle

Order of work

Use the no. 5 crewel needle for the
centres of the flowers and the no. 10
crewel needle for all other embroidery.

Flowers

Each petal is a granitos of four straight
stitches that share the same holes at
the tip and base of the petal. Work
three petals in a 'Y' shape, leaving a
tiny space between the petals. Fill in
the remaining two petals. Surround
each petal with a fly stitch, anchoring it
at the tip. Add a colonial knot to the
centre of each flower.

Stem and buds

Work the stem in stem stitch.
Beginning at the base of the stem,
embroider two colonial knots. Remove
one strand of A from the needle and
leave it dangling on the back of the
fabric. Work the third bud with a
colonial knot and the fourth bud with
a French knot. Remove the remaining
strand of A from the needle and leave it
dangling as before.
 Stitch a colonial knot for the
fifth bud. Work five French knots for
the remaining buds. End off all threads
on the back of the fabric.
 Embroider fly stitches around the
three largest buds, taking the anchoring
stitches into the stem.

Leaves

Stitch a granitos of three straight
stitches for each leaf. Surround these
with detached chains with long
anchoring stitches.

Embroidery key

*All embroidery is worked with two strands
of thread unless otherwise specified.*

Flowers

Petals = B (granitos), B (1 strand, fly stitch)

Centres = C (6 strands, colonial knot)

Stem and buds

Stem = D (1 strand, stem stitch)

Two largest buds = A blended with D (2
strands of each, colonial knot), D (1 strand,
fly stitch)

Third largest bud = 1 strand of A blended with
2 strands of D (colonial knot), D (1 strand,
fly stitch)

Fourth largest bud = 1 strand of A blended
with 2 strands of D (French knot, 1 wrap)

Fifth largest bud = D (colonial knot)

Small buds = D (French knot, 1 wrap)

Leaves = D (granitos, detached chain)

FORGET-ME-NOT

Myosotis sylvatica by Heather Scott

This design uses

Fly stitch, French knot, Granitos, Padded satin stitch,
Satin stitch, Stem stitch, Straight stitch

Embroidery key

All embroidery is worked with one strand of thread unless otherwise specified.

Flowers

Petals = F (2 strands, granitos)

Centres = D (2 strands, French knot, 1 wrap)

Buds = E (padded satin stitch)

Bud calyxes = A (2 strands, fly stitch)

Stems = A (stem stitch)

Leaves = A (satin stitch, stem stitch)

Ladybird

Body = C (satin stitch)

Head = B (satin stitch)

Spots = B (French knot, 1 wrap)

Legs = B (straight stitch)

Forget-me-not – True love. **The Language of Flowers**

Requirements

Threads

DMC stranded cotton

A = 122 variegated leaf green
B = 310 black
C = 321 vy lt garnet
D = 726 golden yellow
E = 798 dk delft
F = 809 delft

Needle

No. 10 sharp needle

Order of work

Stems and leaves

Stitch the stems in stem stitch and the leaves in satin stitch. When working the leaves, complete one half before beginning the next. Partially outline the lower left leaf in stem stitch.

Flowers

Work five petals for each flower. Each petal is a granitos of 5–7 straight stitches. Add a yellow French knot to the centre of each flower.

Beginning at the top and working towards the base, stitch the petals of the buds in padded satin stitch. Embroider a fly stitch around each bud to form the calyx and link the bud to the adjacent stem.

Ladybird

Stitch the head and body with vertical satin stitches. Add three French knots over the previous stitching for the spots. Finally, work two pairs of tiny angled straight stitches for the legs.

FORGET-ME-NOT

Myosotis sylvatica by Margo Fanning

Requirements

Threads

Appletons 2 ply crewel wool
A = 333 lt drab green
B = 343 lt mid olive green
C = 462 lt cornflower
D = 463 cornflower
E = 471 ultra lt autumn yellow
F = 604 mauve
G = 965 iron grey
H = 998 charcoal

Needle

No. 24 chenille needle

Order of work

Use the photograph as a guide to yarn colour changes within the design.

Stems and leaves

Using the drab green yarn, stitch all stems except the section between the two leaves on the middle stem. Work this with the olive green yarn. Embroider rows of stem stitch close together to fill the leaves. Use the drab green yarn for all the leaves except the second lowest leaf, where both greens are used.

Flowers

Stitch the petals of the flowers, using three straight stitches, worked side by side, for each one. Add tiny straight stitch markings to some of the petals on the right hand side of the sprig. Stitch a single French knot in the centre of each flower.

At the tips of the stems, work the bud petals in straight stitch. Partially surround each one with a fly stitch, linking it to the stem.

Bee

Work straight stitches across the body for padding. Cover the padding with six rows of satin stitch, alternating between the charcoal and yellow yarns.

Outline the wings and the division between the thorax and abdomen using back stitch. Add straight stitches to the wings, partially filling them in. Work two straight stitches for each antenna and two for each eye. Using the charcoal yarn, work the legs in back stitch. Add grey straight stitches to some of the segments.

This design uses

Back stitch, Fly stitch, French knot, Padded satin stitch, Stem stitch, Straight stitch

Embroidery key

All embroidery is worked with one strand of yarn unless otherwise specified.

Flowers

Petals = C (straight stitch)

Petal markings = F (straight stitch)

Centres = E (French knot, 1 wrap)

Buds = C or D (straight stitch)

Bud calyxes = A (fly stitch)

Stems = A or B (stem stitch)

Leaves = A and B (stem stitch)

Bee

Body = E and H (padded satin stitch)

Wings = G (back stitch, straight stitch)

Outline between abdomen and thorax = G (back stitch)

Eyes = G and H (straight stitch)

Antennae = G and H (straight stitch)

Legs = H (back stitch), G (straight stitch)

FOXGLOVE

Digitalis purpurea by Carolyn Pearce

Requirements

Threads & ribbons

DMC stranded cotton
A = 225 ultra lt shell pink
B = 3052 med green-grey
C = 3053 green-grey
D = 3354 lt dusky rose
Glen Lorin hand dyed silk ribbon 7mm (⁵⁄₁₆″) wide
E = rippon

Needles

No. 10 crewel needle
No. 12 sharp needle
No. 18 chenille needle

Supplies

Water-soluble fabric

Order of work

Use the sharp needle for the mouths of the flowers and for the sepals, the chenille needle for the leaves and the crewel needle for all other embroidery.

The spires are stitched onto the water-soluble fabric and then attached to the main fabric.

Begin each new thread with a waste knot approx 7.5cm (3″) away. These will later be used to attach the spire to the fabric. As you stitch, allow the threads to crisscross on the back of the fabric. This helps to ensure the stitching does not unravel.

Stems

Stretch the water-soluble fabric tightly into a hoop. Stitch the stems in chain stitch and whip them with the same thread.

Flowers

Begin at the base of the stem and work upwards, gradually decreasing the size of the flowers and weaving the thread through the stem as you move to the position of the next flower. Stitch a detached chain and then a blanket stitch into it for the petals of each flower (*see diag., above, left*). Embroider two fly stitches, which form a circle, for each mouth. Add a green fly stitch to the base for the sepals. Ensure the fly stitches split the previous stitching to keep them secure.

Cut around the embroidery and soak it for a few minutes in cold water. Dry and gently shape the spires.

To attach the spires, take the tails of thread to the back of the fabric and pin the spires in place. Using the tails of thread, secure the spires with tiny stab stitches through the stems.

Buds and leaves

At the top of the spire, embroider a mix of colonial and French knots for the buds. Stitch 4–5 ribbon stitch leaves around the base of each plant.

This design uses

Blanket stitch, Colonial knot, Detached chain, Fly stitch, French knot, Ribbon stitch, Whipped chain stitch

Embroidery key

All thread embroidery is worked with two strands unless otherwise specified.

Flowers

Petals = D (detached chain, blanket stitch)

Mouths = A (1 strand, fly stitch)

Sepals = B (1 strand, fly stitch)

Buds on left spire = A, B and D (colonial knot, French knot, 1 wrap)

Buds on right spire = A, C and D (colonial knot, French knot, 1 wrap)

Stems

Left stem = B (whipped chain stitch)

Right stem = C (whipped chain stitch)

Leaves = E (ribbon stitch)

Foxgloves improve the health of most plants grown nearby.

FRANGIPANI

Plumeria alba by Di Kirchner

This design uses

Bullion knot, Detached chain, Straight stitch

Requirements

Threads

DMC stranded cotton
A = 611 dk taupe
B = 743 yellow
C = 745 vy lt yellow

Needles

No. 9 crewel needle
No. 9 straw (milliner's) needle

Order of work

Stitch the main stem first and then the shorter stems. Work the flowers, using five detached chains for the petals of the whole flowers and 2–3 detached chains for the petals of the partial flowers. Allow some petals to overlap the stems. Add a single straight stitch inside each detached chain.

Making potpourri

Preserve the wonderful fragrance of flowers.

Gather fresh flowers and petals at noon on a dry day. Separate the petals, spread them on wine trays in a well-ventilated room and leave them to dry. Don't be tempted to mix your potpourri until every petal is dry or you'll risk mildew ruining the whole batch.

Blend the dry petals with powdered orris root (1 tablespoon to every 3 cups of petals) and add a few drops of your favourite scented oil. When the scent fades, add a few drops of oil and toss.

Embroidery key

All embroidery is worked with one strand of thread unless otherwise specified.

Flowers = C (2 strands, detached chain), B (straight stitch)

Stems = A (7 bullion knots, 12–40 wraps)

FUCHSIA

Fuchsia 'Tom Thumb' by Angela Dower

Requirements

Threads & ribbons

DMC stranded cotton
A = 326 vy deep rose
B = 745 vy lt yellow
C = 815 dk garnet
D = 3781 dk putty groundings
E = 3834 dk grape
Madeira stranded silk
F = 1603 lt khaki green
YLI silk floss
G = 157 med olive green
Glen Lorin hand dyed silk ribbon 4mm (³⁄₁₆″) wide
H = green sands
Glen Lorin hand dyed silk ribbon 7mm (⁵⁄₁₆″) wide
I = green sands
Colour Streams hand dyed silk ribbon 4mm (³⁄₁₆″) wide
J = poppy
Colour Streams hand dyed silk ribbon 7mm (⁵⁄₁₆″) wide
K = plum

Needles

No. 9 sharp needle
No. 18 chenille needle
No. 20 chenille needle
No. 26 tapestry needle

This design uses
Couching, Fly stitch, Granitos, Loop stitch, Ribbon stitch, Seed stitch, Straight stitch, Twisted fly stitch, Twisted detached chain, Whipped back stitch

Order of work

Use the tapestry needle for the whipping and the sharp needle for all other thread embroidery. Use the no. 18 chenille needle when working with the 7mm (⁵⁄₁₆") ribbon and the no. 20 chenille needle when working with the 4mm (³⁄₁₆") ribbon.

Stems

Stitch all the stems in back stitch. Work a second line of back stitch close to the first along the section between the base and the position of the large leaves. Whip the main stems with the garnet thread and the flower and bud stems with the khaki green thread. Whip the main stems again using the putty coloured thread.

Flowers

Embroider two overlapping loop stitches for the petals of each flower. Fold the loops downwards and couch the underside in place.

Work a small twisted detached chain above the petals. Stitch the side sepals, folding the ribbon before anchoring it. To begin the front sepal, bring the ribbon to the front above the twisted detached chain. Couch the ribbon along both sides of the twisted detached chain. Fold the ribbon and complete the ribbon stitch. Couch the sepals in place.

Stitch straight stitches of varying lengths for the stamens. Work a fly stitch with a very long anchoring stitch for the stigma. At the end, stitch a granitos of eight straight stitches.

Add a tiny straight stitch to the tip. Embroider seed stitches at the ends of the stamens.

Using the narrow green ribbon, work a small twisted detached chain above the pink sepals for the receptacle. Cover it with a straight stitch.

Buds

Each bud is worked in a similar manner. Work a twisted detached chain to form the padding of the lowest segment. Cover this with a straight stitch and couch along the sides. On the pink buds, work a straight stitch in the same ribbon directly above the first stitch. Work the last segment, linking the bud to the stem.

Leaves

Stitch five large leaves with straight stitches and one large leaf with a twisted ribbon stitch. Work the small leaves with ribbon stitches. Anchor the leaves to the stems with single straight stitches. Finally, embroider a twisted fly stitch at the tip of each large leaf.

Embroidery key

All thread embroidery is worked with one strand.

Flowers

Petals = K (loop stitch), A (couching)

Sepals = J (twisted detached chain, ribbon stitch), A (couching)

Stamens = A (straight stitch), E (seed stitch)

Stigmas = A (fly stitch, straight stitch), B (granitos)

Receptacles = H (twisted detached chain, straight stitch)

Pink buds

Sepals = J (twisted detached chain, straight stitch), A (couching)

Receptacles = H (twisted detached chain, straight stitch), G (couching)

Green buds = H (twisted detached chain, straight stitch), G (couching)

Foliage

Main stems = A, D and F (whipped back stitch)

Leaf stems = C (straight stitch)

Flower and bud stems = F (whipped back stitch)

Large leaves = I (straight stitch), G (twisted fly stitch)

Small leaves = H (ribbon stitch)

It is at the edge of the petal that love waits.   *William Carlos Williams*

GERANIUM

Pelargonium 'robe' by Kris Richards

This design uses

Back stitch, Blanket stitch, Detached chain,
Fly stitch, Granitos, Stem stitch, Straight stitch

Embroidery key

All embroidery is worked with two strands of thread unless otherwise specified.

Flowers

Upper and mid right flowers = A
(detached chain)

Mid left flowers = B (detached chain)

Lower flowers = C (detached chain)

Buds = A, B or C (granitos)

Foliage

Main stems = E (stem stitch)

Stems to leaves = E (1 strand, stem stitch)

Stems to flowers = E (straight stitch)

Bud calyxes and stems = E (fly stitch)

Leaves = E (1 strand, blanket stitch)

Terra cotta pot

Outline = D (back stitch)

Shading = D (1 strand, straight stitch)

Requirements

Threads

DMC stranded cotton
A = 321 vy lt garnet
B = 349 dk coral
C = 666 bright Christmas red
D = 921 copper
E = 3012 med khaki green

Needle

No. 8 crewel needle

Order of work

Foliage

Embroider the main stems and leaf stems in stem stitch. Work straight stitches for the smaller stems to the flowers and a fly stitch for the calyx and stem of each bud. Stitch the leaves in blanket stitch, keeping the stitches close together and all beginning from the same hole in the fabric.

Flowers

Using the photograph as a guide to thread colour changes, work a group of 3–5 tiny detached chains for the petals of each flower. Begin with the darkest red thread at the top and work through to the brightest red thread for the lower flowers. Embroider a granitos of 2–3 straight stitches for each bud.

Pot

Outline the pot in back stitch. Fill in the shadow areas of the pot with horizontal straight stitches of varying lengths.

GERANIUM

Geranium renardii by Susan O'Connor

This design uses

Back stitch, Encroaching stem stitch, Long and short stitch,
Satin stitch, Seed stitch, Straight stitch

Requirements

Threads

Madeira stranded silk

A = 0506 raspberry pink
B = 0812 med shell pink
C = 0813 lt shell pink
D = 0815 vy lt shell pink
E = 1508 olive green
F = 1603 lt khaki green
G = 2208 lt old gold

Needle

No. 12 sharp needle

Order of work

Embroider the petals in long and short
stitch using the lighter pink on the
outer sections and the darker pink
nearer the centre. Work the petal
markings over the previous stitching.
Fill the centre with pale green
satin stitches. Add tiny seed stitches
for the yellow specks.

Work both the petals and sepals
of the buds in satin stitch.

Embroider the stems with
encroaching stem stitch and then
fill the leaves with long and short
stitch. Finally, work the leaf veins
and all outlines.

Botanica, Inspirations 22

To her let us garlands bring.   *William Shakespeare*

GERBERA

Gerbera jamesonii by Di Kirchner

This design uses
Detached chain, French knot,
Stem stitch, Straight stitch

Requirements

Threads

DMC stranded cotton
A = 208 dk lavender
B = 602 med cranberry
C = 741 med tangerine
D = 745 vy lt yellow
E = 987 forest green

Needle
No. 9 crewel needle

Order of work

Embroider the flower petals first,
working 16–18 for each flower.
  Stitch a detached chain with a
straight stitch inside it to create
each petal. Fill the centre with a cluster
of tightly packed French knots.
  Work the stems in stem stitch.

Embroidery key

*All embroidery is worked with one strand
of thread unless otherwise specified.*

Flowers

Petals = A, B or C (detached chain,
straight stitch)

Centres = D (French knot, 1 wrap)

Stems = E (2 strands, stem stitch)

GRAPE HYACINTH

Muscari botryoides by Joan Gibson

This design uses
French knot, Straight stitch

Requirements

Threads

DMC stranded cotton
A = 368 lt pistachio green
B = 792 dk cornflower blue

Needle
No. 9 crewel needle

Order of work

Work the stems and leaves in straight
stitch. Embroider groups of seven
French knots around the top of each
stem for the flowers.

Embroidery key

*All embroidery is worked with one strand of
thread unless otherwise specified.*

Flowers = B (2 strands, French knot, 1 wrap)

Stems = A (straight stitch)

Leaves = A (straight stitch)

They open very deliberately and there abide for a little while. *E.V. Boyle*

GUM BLOSSOM

Eucalyptus ficifolia by Joan Gibson

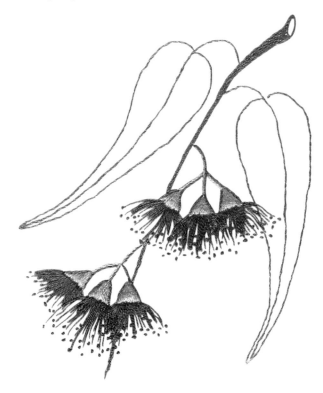

This design uses

Couching, French knot, Padded satin stitch, Stem stitch, Straight stitch

Embroidery key

All embroidery is worked with one strand of thread.

Flowers

Flower stems = B and E (stem stitch)

Cups = B (padded satin stitch)

Cup outlines = E (stem stitch)

Stamens = D (straight stitch, couching, French knot, 1 wrap)

Main stem = C (stem stitch)

Leaves = A (stem stitch)

Eucalypts are also naturally found in the Philippines, Malaysia, Indonesia, Papua New Guinea and Melanesia.

Requirements

Threads

DMC stranded cotton

A = 522 fern green
B = 543 ultra lt beige
C = 841 lt beige
D = 3712 med salmon
E = 3778 lt terra cotta

Needle

No. 9 crewel needle

Order of work

Main stem and leaves

Outline the main stem in stem stitch and then fill it in with closely worked rows of stem stitch. Change to the green thread and embroider the leaves in stem stitch.

Flowers

Embroider the outer flowers in each group before the central one. Work 2–3 straight stitches across each cup for padding. Fill the cups with vertical satin stitches and work the flower stems with the same thread. Using the terra cotta thread, outline the cups and finish the flower stems with stem stitch.

Embroider the stamens next, beginning at the middle of one cup. Work two straight stitches, which use the same holes in the fabric and then a French knot at the end. On each side of this, work single straight stitches of varying lengths. Couch the longer stitches in place. Stitch French knots near the tips of the straight stitches. Work the remaining flowers in the same manner, making the stamens of the central flowers a little longer than those of the side flowers.

GYPSOPHILA

Gypsophila elegans by Di Kirchner

This design uses
Fly stitch, French knot, Straight stitch

Requirements

Threads
DMC stranded cotton
A = blanc
B = 3347 med yellow-green

Needle
No. 9 crewel needle

Order of work

Stitch a straight stitch for the tip of
one stem. Directly below the straight
stitch, work a fly stitch with a long
anchoring stitch. Continue working
fly stitches, one directly below the
other, until reaching the base of
the stem. Repeat for the
remaining stems.

Work white French knots at the tip
of the straight stitch and at the tips of
the 'arms' of the fly stitches.

The beauty of flowers

The most durable and
costly materials the earth
holds in her bosom, stone
and marble, gold, and silver,
and gems, have been made
to assume, in a thousand
imposing or graceful forms, the
lines of the living vegetation. How
very many of the proudest works
of art would be wanting, if there
had been no grace and dignity
in trees, no beauty in leaves
and flowers!

Rural Hours,
by Susan Fenimore Cooper

Embroidery key

*All embroidery is worked with one strand
of thread unless otherwise specified.*

Flowers = A (2 strands, French knot,
1 wrap)

Stems = B (fly stitch, straight stitch)

HIBISCUS

Hibiscus rosa-sinensis by Di Kirchner

This design uses
Detached chain, French knot, Granitos, Stem stitch, Straight stitch

Requirements

Threads

DMC stranded cotton
A = 349 dk coral
B = 745 vy lt yellow
C = 962 med dusky rose
D = 963 ultra lt dusky rose
E = 987 forest green

Needle

No. 9 sharp needle

Each flower is a soul blossoming
out to nature. *Gerard de Nerval*

Order of work

Flowers

Stitch a granitos of four straight stitches for each petal. Surround each one with a detached chain. Pull the thread gently and ensure the detached chain lies around the granitos and not over it.

On the pink hibiscus, add a straight stitch to each petal for markings. Work a straight stitch and then a tiny cluster of French knots at the tip for the stamen.

On the red hibiscus, work a straight stitch and two French knots at the tip in the red thread. Stitch a cluster of tiny yellow French knots along the straight stitch.

Stems and leaves

Embroider the stems in stem stitch. Work a detached chain for each leaf and place a straight stitch inside it.

The heart of a flower

When at last I took the time to look into the heart of a flower, it opened up a whole new world… as if a window had been opened to let in the sun.

Princess Grace of Monaco

Embroidery key

All embroidery is worked with two strands of thread unless otherwise specified.

Flowers

Petals = A or D (granitos)

Petal outlines = A or D (detached chain)

Petal markings on pink flower = C (straight stitch)

Stamen on pink flower = C (straight stitch), B (1 strand, French knot, 1 wrap)

Stamen on red flower = A (straight stitch, French knot, 1 wrap), B (1 strand, French knot, 1 wrap)

Stems = E (stem stitch)

Leaves = E (detached chain, straight stitch)

HOLLYHOCK

Alcea rosea by Carolyn Pearce

This design uses
Colonial knot,
French knot, Ruching, Smocker's knot,
Stem stitch, Straight stitch,
Twisted detached chain

Requirements

Threads & ribbons

Madeira stranded silk
A = 1704 dk blue-green
DMC stranded cotton
B = 676 lt old gold
Faveur variegated ribbon 4mm (³⁄₁₆") wide
C = 11 deep apricot
D = 24 soft apricot
YLI silk ribbon 4mm (³⁄₁₆") wide
E = 33 dk blue-green

Needles

No. 22 chenille needle
No. 18 chenille needle
No. 12 sharp needle
No. 8 crewel needle

Supplies

Water-soluble fabric marker
Apricot machine sewing thread

*And 'tis my faith that
every flower / Enjoys the air
it breathes.* **William Wordsworth**

Order of work

Use the sharp needle for stitching the flowers and the no. 18 chenille needle for attaching them. Work all other ribbon embroidery with the no. 22 chenille needle and thread embroidery with the crewel needle.

Stem and leaves

Stitch the stem in stem stitch. Work a twisted detached chain for each leaf. Add a smocker's knot to the base and a straight stitch to the tip of each one.

Flowers

Stitch the flowers following the step-by-step instructions on page 45. Make three with the soft apricot ribbon and eight with the deep apricot ribbon.

Attach the darker flowers to the lower section of the plant and the lighter ones to the upper section. At the very top, work three colonial knot buds with the soft apricot ribbon. Using the green thread, stitch seven colonial knots among the ribbon buds and three French knots above them.

Embroidery key

All thread embroidery is worked with one strand unless otherwise specified.

Flowers

Petals = C or D (ruching)

Centres = B (3 strands, colonial knot)

Large buds = D (colonial knot)

Small buds = A (colonial knot, French knot, 1 wrap)

Stem = A (stem stitch)

Leaves = E (twisted detached chain), A (straight stitch, smocker's knot)

STEP-BY-STEP HOLLYHOCK

We used wider ribbon for photographic purposes.

1 Cut 9cm (3½″) of ribbon. Mark palest edge 2cm (¾″) in from each end using fabric marker. Mark distance between at 1cm (⅜″) intervals.

2 Knot a length of machine sewing thread. Work a back stitch at the first mark.

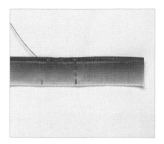

3 Work running stitches almost to opposite side. Rounding corner, change direction and stitch close to the edge until almost opposite the second mark.

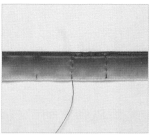

4 Round the corner again and stitch to the opposite edge. Finish with the thread at the back of the ribbon.

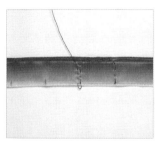

5 Bring the thread over the edge of the ribbon and stitch back towards the opposite side.

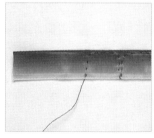

6 Continue in this manner to the last mark on the ribbon.

7 Hold the ribbon between your fingers to prevent it twisting and pull up the running stitches firmly.

8 Secure the thread but do not cut it off. Bring the two knots together and take the thread through the starting knot.

9 Place the large chenille needle in the fabric. Thread the tails of ribbon and thread into the needle.

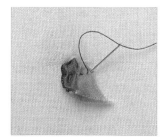

10 Pull tails to back of fabric. Remove chenille needle. Trim ribbon tails at an angle. Use the thread to secure the tails.

11 Take the thread to the front. Secure the flower with tiny stab stitches in the folds of the ribbon close to the centre.

12 Work a colonial knot at the centre of the flower.

45

HYDRANGEA

Hydrangea macrophylla by Angela Dower

This design uses

Blanket stitch, Detached chain, Fly stitch,
French knot, Looped straight stitch, Stem stitch

Requirements

Threads & Ribbons

Madeira stranded silk
A = 1407 avocado green
B = 1408 lt avocado green
C = 1602 dk khaki green
D = 1603 lt khaki green
Madeira Decora stranded rayon
E = 1480 med violet
F = 1543 vy dk cornflower blue
Glen Lorin hand dyed silk ribbon 4mm (³⁄₁₆″) wide
G = primrose
YLI silk ribbon 4mm (³⁄₁₆″) wide
H = 117 hyacinth

Needles

No. 18 chenille needle
No. 8 straw (milliner's) needle

Supplies

Jo Sonja fabric medium
Jo Sonja acrylic artists' paints red, blue, white and green
Fine paintbrush

Order of work

Use the chenille needle for the ribbon embroidery and the straw needle for the thread embroidery.

Use the photograph as a guide to thread and ribbon colour changes within the design.

Painting

Paint the flower heads. Mix the fabric medium with the paints until you achieve the desired colour. Test the colour on a scrap of fabric before applying it to the design. Using the green paint, repeat the procedure for the leaves.

Stems

Stitch the main stem with rows of stem stitch side by side. Begin each row at the base of the stem and grade the colours from the lightest green on the left to the darkest on the right. Embroider the flower and leaf stems with single rows of stem stitch.

Work a tiny detached chain in the centre of the main stem's base. Surround this with a second detached chain. Continue in this manner until the base is complete.

Leaves

Stitch the leaf veins in stem stitch. Keeping the 'purl' of the stitches along the edges of the leaves, fill the leaves with blanket stitch. Work the folded sections of the leaves separately.

Flowers

Beginning at the top and working downwards, embroider the petals of the flowers with looped straight stitch. Vary the angles of the petals. Fill any spaces with green fly stitches or partial flowers using 1–3 looped straight stitches. Leave some background paint exposed in parts. This will give the flower heads added depth.

Using blended threads, work single French knots for the centres.

Avoid placing flowers in direct sunlight. It will bleach the colour from dried flowers and cause fresh flowers to mature too quickly.

Embroidery key

All thread embroidery is worked with one strand unless otherwise specified.

Flowers
Petals = G and H (looped straight stitch)
Centres = E blended with F (1 strand of each, French knot, 1 wrap)

Stems and leaves
Main stem = A, B, C and D (stem stitch)

Base of main stem = B (detached chain)
Flower and leaf stems = A, B, C and D (stem stitch)
Tiny stems = B and D (fly stitch)
Leaves = A, B, C and D (blanket stitch)
Leaf veins = B and D (stem stitch)

HYDRANGEA

Hydrangea macrophylla by Kris Richards

This design uses

Back stitch, Fly stitch, French knot

Requirements

Threads

DMC stranded cotton
A = 317 pewter grey
B = 3011 dk khaki green
C = 3051 dk green-grey
Needle Necessities overdyed floss
D = 149 hydrangea

Needles

No. 1 straw (milliner's) needle
No. 8 crewel needle

Order of work

Use the straw needle for working the French knots and the crewel needle for all other embroidery.

Stitch the urn in back stitch. Work the fly stitch leaves following the step-by-step instructions on page 49.

When stitching the hydrangeas, complete one ball of flowers before starting the next. Begin working the French knots around the edge of the flower ball, keeping them packed tightly together.

Hydrangeas add a wonderful show of colour to a shady corner of the garden. They range in colours from blue, mauve, pink and red and it is possible to change from one colour range to another by adding chemicals to the soil. Lime added to the soil turns them pink and aluminium sulphate turns them blue. In Australia, hydrangea flowers are often dried and used as Christmas decorations.

Embroidery key

All embroidery is worked with one strand of thread unless otherwise specified.

Flowers = D (4 strands, French knot, 2 wraps)

Leaves = B or C (fly stitch)

Urn = A (back stitch)

STEP-BY-STEP FLY STITCH LEAF

1 **Leaf curling to the left.** Bring the thread to the front at A, a short distance from tip of leaf. Hold it to the left.

2 Take the needle from B to C. A, B and C are aligned and B is at the tip of the leaf.

3 Pull the thread through, ensuring it goes under tip of needle. Take the needle to the back of the fabric just over the loop of thread.

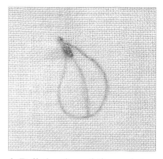

4 Pull the thread through to anchor the loop.

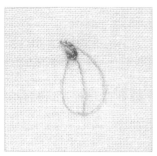

5 Work a second fly stitch around the first.

6 Work several more fly stitches in the same manner until the leaf is the desired width.

7 Work the next fly stitch directly below the previous stitch. This stitch is the same width as the previous one.

8 Continue working stitches following step 7 until the leaf is the desired length.

9 End off the last stitch.

10 **Leaf curling to the right.** Bring the thread to the front at A. Hold it to the right and take the needle from B to C.

11 Work the stitches in the same manner but as a mirror image of those for a leaf curling to the left.

HONEYSUCKLE

Lonicera etrusca by Carol Hawkins

This design uses

Couching, Encroaching stem stitch,
French knot, Long and short stitch,
Satin stitch, Straight stitch

Requirements

Threads

DMC stranded cotton
A = 434 lt brown
B = 435 vy lt brown
C = 580 dk moss green
D = 581 moss green
E = 680 dk old gold
Madeira stranded silk
F = 0112 custard
G = 2207 vy lt old gold
H = 2208 lt old gold
I = 2209 med old gold
**Minnamurra hand dyed
stranded cotton**
J = 180 straw yellow/green

Needle

No. 10 sharp needle

Order of work

Use the photograph as a guide
to thread colour changes within
the design.

Stem and leaves

Starting at the base, stitch the stem in
satin stitch. Gradually change to
encroaching stem stitch as you near
the tip.

Using the two shades of moss
green, embroider the leaves in
satin stitch. Work along one half of
the leaf, around the tip and then down
the other half.

Flowers

Beginning at the base, work the petals
of the open flowers in satin stitch and
long and short stitch. Embroider 5–6
straight stitches of varying lengths for
the stamens. Couch some stamens to
achieve a gentle curve. Add a tiny
straight stitch across the top of
each one.

Work the closed flowers in
satin stitch. Embroider tightly packed
French knots where the base of the
flowers join the stem.

Embroidery key

All embroidery is worked with one strand of thread.

Flowers

Petals of open flowers = B, E, G, H, I and J (satin stitch, long and short stitch)

Petals of closed flowers = G, H, I and J (satin stitch)

Stamens = F and I (straight stitch)

Base of flowers = B, E, G, H and J (French knot, 1 wrap)

Stem = A (satin stitch, encroaching stem stitch)

Leaves = C or D (satin stitch)

HYACINTH

Hyacinthus orientalis by Di Kirchner

This design uses
French knot, stem stitch

Requirements

Threads

DMC stranded cotton
A = 962 med dusky rose
B = 963 ultra lt dusky rose
C = 3346 hunter green

Needle

No. 9 sharp needle

Order of work

Using blended threads, embroider French knots very close together to form the flower heads. Stitch the stems and leaves in stem stitch.

Embroidery key

All embroidery is worked with two strands of thread.

Flowers = A blended with B (1 strand of each, French knot, 1 wrap)

Stems = C (stem stitch)

Leaves = C (stem stitch)

HYACINTH

Hyacinthus orientalis by Joan Gibson

This design uses
French knot, straight stitch

Requirements

Threads

DMC stranded cotton
A = 813 lt blue
B = 827 vy lt blue
C = 828 ultra lt blue
D = 3347 med yellow-green

Needle

No. 10 crewel needle

Order of work

Beginning at the top with the darkest shade of blue and grading to the lightest shade at the bottom, stitch a mass of tightly clustered French knots. Add long straight stitches for the leaves and stems.

Embroidery key

All embroidery is worked with one strand of thread.

Flowers

Upper flowers = A (French knot, 2 wraps)

Middle flowers = B (French knot, 2 wraps)

Lower flowers = C (French knot, 2 wraps)

Stems = D (straight stitch)

Leaves = D (straight stitch)

IRIS

Iris species by Angela Dower

This design uses
Couching, Ribbon stitch, Straight stitch,
Twisted detached chain, Whipped back stitch,

Embroidery key

All thread embroidery is worked with one strand.

Flowers

Petals = D (ribbon stitch, straight stitch), B (couching)

Calyx on lower right iris = C (straight stitch)

Bud = D (twisted detached chain)

Bud calyx = C (straight stitch)

Stems = A (whipped back stitch)

Leaves = C (ribbon stitch), A (couching)

Requirements

Threads & ribbons

Madeira stranded silk
A = 1603 khaki green
YLI silk floss
B = 157 drab olive
Glen Lorin hand dyed silk ribbon 4mm (³⁄₁₆″) wide
C = green sands
Colour Streams hand dyed silk ribbon 7mm (⁵⁄₁₆″) wide
D = wisteria

Needles

No. 9 sharp needle
No. 26 tapestry needle
No. 18 chenille needle
No. 20 chenille needle

Order of work

Use the tapestry needle for the whipping and the sharp needle for all other thread embroidery. Use the no. 22 chenille needle for the 4mm (³⁄₁₆″) ribbon and the no. 20 chenille needle for the 7mm (⁵⁄₁₆″) ribbon.

Stems and leaves

Stitch the stems for the two lower flowers. Work the leaves and then the two remaining stems. Couch the leaves at their folds.

Iris – Message. *The Language of Flowers*

Flowers

Stitch the flowers following the step-by-step instructions on page 53. When working the lower right flower, stitch the last petal so it overlaps the previous upper petals.

Add a short straight stitch at the base to form a calyx.

Bud

Embroider a twisted detached chain for the petals of the bud. Using the green ribbon and beginning at the base of the petals, stitch two straight stitches which overlap and finish approximately two thirds of the way up on the sides of the petals. Add a short straight stitch across the bottom of the two previous straight stitches.

STEP-BY-STEP IRIS

1 **Stem.** Work the stem in back stitch. Whip it with the same thread, taking the needle under each back stitch.

2 **Leaves.** Work long ribbon stitches, adding a fold or twist to some of the stitches.

3 Couch the ribbon wherever there is a fold or twist.

4 **Flower.** Mark the centre. Work a ribbon stitch directly above the mark.

5 Bring the ribbon to the front on one side of the mark. Fold it and then complete the ribbon stitch. Take care to keep the ribbon loose. Repeat on the opposite side.

6 Beginning on each side of the centre mark, work two loose ribbon stitches which overlap the first stitch. Ensure the tips of the stitches touch.

7 Beginning directly below the upper petals, work a straight stitch. (On the lower right iris, this stitch is worked over the upper petals rather than downwards.)

8 Couch the side petals in place at the folds.

Orris root

When making potpourri, a fixative is needed to hold or preserve the fragrance. A commonly used fixative is powdered orris root. This is the diced and crushed rhizome of the bearded iris. Hang pieces of rhizome in a well-ventilated place until they are dry. Crush or grind them into a powder and store in a dark glass container.

IRIS

Iris species by Di Kirchner

This design uses
Detached chain, French knot, Stem stitch

Requirements

Threads

DMC stranded cotton
A = 211 lt lavender
B = 368 lt pistachio green
C = 743 yellow

Needle

No. 9 crewel needle

Order of work

Stitch three detached chains for the upper petals and two for the lower petals. Work a very tiny detached chain for the bud. Add a single French knot to the centre of the flower. Using single rows of stem stitch, work the main stem and the stem to the bud.

Stitch two rows of stem stitch, side by side, for the leaves.

Embroidery key

All embroidery is worked with two strands of thread unless otherwise specified.

Flower

Petals = A (detached chain)

Centre = C (1 strand, French knot, 1 wrap)

Bud = A (detached chain)

Stems and leaves = B (stem stitch)

IMPATIENS

Impatiens walleriana by Di Kirchner

This design uses
Detached chain, French knot, Straight stitch

Requirements

Threads

Anchor stranded cotton
A = 335 bright orange-red
DMC stranded cotton
B = 746 off-white
C = 987 forest green

Needle

No. 9 sharp needle

Order of work

Work six detached chains for the petals of each flower. Add a single French knot to the centre of each one.

Scatter leaves around the outer edge of the group of flowers. For each leaf, embroider a detached chain and place a straight stitch inside the loop.

Embroidery key

All embroidery is worked with two strands of thread unless otherwise specified.

Flowers

Petals = A (detached chain)

Centres = B (1 strand, French knot, 1 wrap)

Leaves = C (detached chain, straight stitch)

JONQUIL

Narcissus jonquilla by Di Kirchner

This design uses
French knot, Stem stitch

Requirements

Threads

DMC stranded cotton
A = 445 lt lemon
B = 746 off-white
C = 986 dk forest green

Needle
No. 9 sharp needle

Order of work

Work the stems and leaves first.
Embroider a tiny circle of six French
knots for the petals of each flower.
Using the lemon thread, work a single
French knot for each centre.

Embroidery key

*All embroidery is worked with two strands
of thread.*

Flowers

Petals = B (French knot, 1 wrap)

Centres = A (French knot, 1 wrap)

Stems and leaves = C (stem stitch)

Jonquils and daffodils

These are amongst the most popular of all spring flowers. Known since the
14th century in England, Narcissus are native to Europe and North Africa and the
genus contains more than 50 species. With a little care when planted, jonquils
and daffodils will grow, flower and multiply every year with very little attention.
They are extremely versatile bulbs, suitable for pots, mixed borders, under trees
and shrubs and 'natural' planting in drifts or banks. Clumps need to be divided
when they become overcrowded as the quality of the flowers will decline. This
should be done after the bulbs have flowered and the leaves have yellowed,
allowing the bulb to store food for the next flowering season.

LAVENDER

Lavandula by Kris Richards

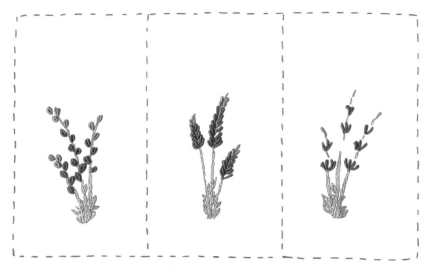

This design uses
Bullion knot, Detached chain, Running stitch, Stem stitch, Straight stitch

Embroidery key

All embroidery is worked with one strand of thread.

Lavender on left

Lower flowers = C (2 bullion knots, 10 wraps)

Upper flowers = D (2 bullion knots, 10 wraps)

Stems = B (stem stitch)

Leaves = B (detached chain)

Lavender in centre

Lower flowers = C (bullion knot, 6–12 wraps)

Upper flowers = D (bullion knot, 5 wraps)

Stems = B (stem stitch)

Leaves = B (detached chain)

Lavender on right

Lower flowers = C (bullion knots, 10 wraps)

Upper flowers = D (bullion knot, 10 wraps)

Stems = B (stem stitch, straight stitch)

Leaves = B (detached chain)

Border = A (running stitch)

Requirements

Threads

DMC stranded cotton

A = 451 dk shell grey
B = 3023 lt Jacobean green
C = 3041 med antique violet
D = 3042 lt antique violet

Needles

No. 8 crewel needle
No. 8 straw (milliner's) needle

Order of work

Use the straw needle for the bullion knots and the crewel needle for all other embroidery.

Lavender on left

Stitch the stems in stem stitch. Cluster detached chains at the base of the stems for the leaves.

Embroider two bullion knots, side by side, for each flower. Use the lighter violet thread for the upper flowers and the darker shade for the lower flowers.

Lavender in centre

Work the stems first, stitching from the base to the bottom of the highest flower. Clump detached chain leaves around the base of the stems.

Beginning at the tip of the stem, stitch a single bullion knot in the lightest shade of violet. Embroider 1–2 pairs of bullion knots directly below in the same thread. Change thread colour and work 5–7 pairs of bullion knots down the stem.

Lavender on right

Using the darker violet thread, stitch groups of 2–4 bullion knots, fanning them from the base. Add a single bullion knot in the lighter violet thread at the tip.

Stitch the lower section of each stem in stem stitch. Work straight stitches between the groups of flowers for the remainder of the stems. Embroider a mass of detached chains at the base of the stems for leaves.

Border

Stitch around the outer edge in running stitch. Work the two internal lines in the same manner.

LILIES

Zantedeschia aethiopica by Di Kirchner

This design uses
Bullion knot, Long and short stitch,
Satin stitch, Stem stitch, Straight stitch

Requirements

Threads

DMC stranded cotton
A = 743 yellow
B = 937 med avocado
C = 3865 winter white

Needles

No. 9 crewel needle
No. 9 straw (milliner's) needle

Order of work

Use the straw needle for the bullion knots and the crewel needle for all other embroidery.

Flowers

Fill the petal shapes with long and short stitch and then outline them with stem stitch.

Work a bullion knot in the lower section of each flower for the stamen.

Stems and leaves

Embroider the leaves in satin stitch, completing one half before beginning the next. Work the stems next. Finish the top of the flower stems with two tiny straight stitches that form a 'V' at the base of the petals.

Embroidery key

All embroidery is worked with one strand of thread unless otherwise specified.

Flowers

Petals = C (long and short stitch)

Petal outlines = C (stem stitch)

Stamens = A (bullion knot, 15 wraps)

Stems = B (2 strands, stem stitch, straight stitch)

Leaves = B (2 strands, satin stitch)

Lilium bulbiferum by Di Kirchner

This design uses
Detached chain, Feather stitch,
Straight stitch

Requirements

Threads

DMC stranded cotton
A = 677 vy lt old gold
B = 722 lt orange spice
C = 921 copper
D = 3347 med yellow-green

Needle

No. 9 crewel needle

Order of work

Stitch the petals first, embroidering three plump detached chains in a 'Y' shape. Place a straight stitch within each detached chain. Work a thinner detached chain in the spaces between.

Using the pale gold thread, work five straight stitches of differing lengths radiating from the centre of the flower for the stamens. These cover one of the petals. Add very tiny straight stitches to the tips of the stamens with the copper thread.

Work a line of single feather stitch for the stem and leaves of each flower.

Embroidery key

All embroidery is worked with two strands of thread unless otherwise specified.

Flowers

Petals = B (detached chain, straight stitch)

Stamens = A and C (1 strand, straight stitch)

Stems and leaves = D (feather stitch)

LILY OF THE VALLEY

Convallaria majalis by Joan Gibson

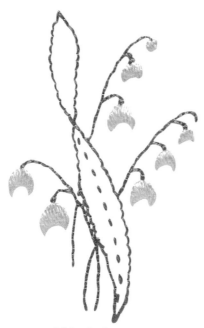

This design uses

Back stitch, Double back stitch, Granitos,
Padded satin stitch, Running stitch,
Straight stitch

Requirements

Threads

DMC stranded cotton
A = 3347 med yellow-green
B = B5200 bright white

Needle

No. 10 crewel needle

Order of work

Leaf

Stitch the leaf vein with running stitch.
Shadow embroider the leaf following
the step-by-step instructions on
page 59.

Flowers

Work 2–3 horizontal straight stitches
within one flower shape for padding.
Beginning at the centre, cover one side
of the flower shape with satin stitch.
Return to the centre and cover the
other side. Stitch the remaining flowers
in the same manner.

Stitch all stems in back stitch.
Embroider a tiny granitos of three
straight stitches at the base of each
flower for the calyx.

Lily of the valley, the national
flower of Finland, means return
of happiness.   *The Language of Flowers*

Embroidery key

*All embroidery is worked with one strand
of thread.*

Leaf

Leaf vein = A (running stitch)

Leaf filling and outline = A (double back stitch)

Flowers

Flower heads = B (padded satin stitch)

Stems = A (back stitch)

Calyxes = A (granitos)

The moral of flowers

Flowers are a delight to every one; to some, perhaps, merely for their beauty
and fragrance; to others, independently of these acknowledged charms, for
the varied pleasurable associations and thoughts they suggest. And foremost
amongst these is the assurance they afford of the exuberant goodness of God.

Rebecca Hey
The Moral of Flowers, 1833

STEP-BY-STEP SHADOW WORKED LEAF

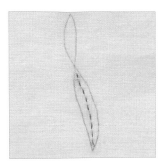

1 Work running stitches along the centre of the leaf for the vein.

2 Begin with a waste knot. Bring thread to front at A, approx 1.5mm (1/16") from tip. Pull through. Take the needle to the back at B.

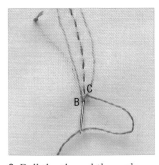

3 Pull the thread through. Re-emerge at C, and pull through. Take the needle to the back at B through the same hole in the fabric.

4 Pull the thread through. Re-emerge at D, approx. 1.5mm (1/16") from A.

5 Pull the thread through. Take the needle to the back at A, through the same hole in the fabric.

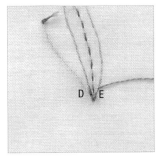

6 Pull the thread through. Re-emerge at E, opposite D.

7 Continue working back stitches, alternating from side to side.

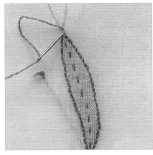

8 **Crossover.** To create the twisting effect, the two lines of stitching cross. Work a back stitch which covers the crossover point.

9 Bring the thread to the front on the opposite line. Work a back stitch that crosses the previous stitch.

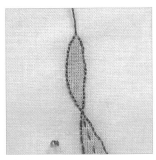

10 Continue working back stitches, alternating from side to side, until reaching the end.

11 To end off, weave the thread through the threads on the wrong side close to the edge.

Completed shadow embroidered leaf worked with double back stitch.

LILY OF THE VALLEY

Convallaria majalis by Margo Fanning

Requirements

Threads

Appletons 2 ply crewel wool
A = 251A ultra lt grass green
B = 301 vy lt red fawn
C = 314 brown olive
D = 343 vy lt mid olive green
E = 901 vy lt golden brown
F = 761 ultra lt biscuit brown
G = 762 vy lt biscuit brown
H = 984 putty groundings
I = 991 white

Needle

No. 24 chenille needle

Order of work

Use the photograph as a guide to yarn colour changes within the design. Work the stems in stem stitch. Add short straight stitches to the stems for the stalks of some of the flowers. Outline the leaves in stem stitch. Fill each leaf with vertical rows of stem stitch, beginning with the centre rows.

Embroider each flower with blanket stitches, fanning the stitches slightly. Using the golden brown yarn, add five colonial knot buds to the tip of the middle stem. Add six buds to the top of the left stem, using both the golden brown and white yarns.

This design uses
Blanket stitch, Colonial knot, Stem stitch, Straight stitch

Embroidery key

All embroidery is worked with one strand of yarn unless otherwise specified.

Flowers = I (blanket stitch)

Buds = E or I (colonial knot)

Stems = E (2 strands, stem stitch)

Left leaf

Outline = H (stem stitch)

Filling = C, D, F, G and H (stem stitch)

Right leaf

Outline = B (stem stitch)

Filling = A, B, C, D and G (stem stitch)

Flowers are the sweetest things God ever made and forgot to put a soul into. *Henry Ward Beecher*

LOBELIA

Lobelia erinus by Di Kirchner

This design uses
Fly stitch, Straight stitch

Requirements

Threads

DMC stranded cotton
A = 333 vy dk blue-violet
B = 3347 med yellow-green

Needle

No. 9 crewel needle

Order of work

Stitch the stems and leaves first. Begin each stem with a straight stitch and then work fly stitches one under the other to the base of the stem. Using the blue-violet thread, embroider tiny fly stitches at the tips of the straight and fly stitches except for the lowest fly stitch of each stem.

Embroidery key

All embroidery is worked with one strand of thread unless otherwise specified.

Flowers = A (2 strands, fly stitch)

Stems and leaves = B (fly stitch, straight stitch)

MARIGOLD

Tagetes erecta by Di Kirchner

This design uses
Detached chain, French knot, Stem stitch, Straight stitch

Requirements

Threads

DMC stranded cotton
A = 742 lt tangerine
B = 3347 med yellow-green

Needle

No. 9 crewel needle

Order of work

Flowers

Work a circle of detached chains to begin the petals of one flower. Stitch a second circle of detached chains over the first, then add a French knot to the centre. Stitch the remaining two flowers in the same manner. Embroider three small detached chains, which share the same hole at the base, for each bud. Work 2–3 tiny straight stitches at the base of each bud to form the calyx.

Stems and leaves

Stitch the flower and leaf stems in stem stitch. Add detached chain leaves along each side of the leaf stems and one at the tip.

Embroidery key

All embroidery is worked with one strand of thread.

Flowers

Petals = A (detached chain)

Centres = A (French knot, 2 wraps)

Buds = A (detached chain)

Bud calyxes = B (straight stitch)

Stems = B (stem stitch)

Leaves = B (detached chain)

NASTURTIUM

Tropaeolum majus by Di Kirchner

This design uses
Blanket stitch, Detached chain,
French knot, Stem stitch, Straight stitch

Requirements

Threads

DMC stranded cotton
A = 608 bright orange
B = 745 vy lt yellow
C = 3347 med yellow-green

Needle

No. 9 crewel needle

Order of work

Flowers

Stitch five detached chains for the petals
of each flower. Place a straight stitch
inside each detached chain. Work single
yellow French knots for the centres.

Stems and leaves

Work the stems to the flowers and leaves
in stem stitch. Embroider each leaf with
radiating blanket stitches which begin
from the same hole in the fabric.

Embroidery key

*All embroidery is worked with one strand
of thread unless otherwise specified.*

Flowers

Petals = A (2 strands, detached chain,
straight stitch)

Centres = B (French knot, 1 wrap)

Stems = C (stem stitch)

Leaves = C (blanket stitch)

ORCHID

Cymbidium by Di Kirchner

This design uses
Detached chain, Straight stitch

Requirements

Threads

DMC stranded cotton
A = 744 lt yellow
B = 921 copper
C = 3013 lt khaki green
D = 3865 winter white

Needle

No. 9 crewel needle

Order of work

Using the green thread, work five
detached chains for the petals of
each flower. Stitch one long straight
stitch for the main stem. Link the flowers
to the main stem with straight stitches.
Take these stitches just over the main
stem so it is anchored to the fabric.

Change to the winter white thread
and work a detached chain inside the
upper petal and one between the two
lower petals of each flower.

Embroider a straight stitch inside
the winter white detached chain with
the yellow thread. Using the
copper thread, place a tiny straight
stitch each side of the yellow stitch.

Embroidery key

*All embroidery is worked with two strands
of thread unless otherwise specified.*

Flowers

Petals = C and D (detached chain)

Petal markings = A (1 strand,
straight stitch), B (straight stitch)

Stems = C (straight stitch)

ORCHID

Cymbidium by Rosemary Frezza

This design uses

Blanket stitch, Couching, French knot, Long and short stitch, Overcast stitch, Satin stitch

Requirements

Threads

DMC stranded cotton
A = 543 ultra lt beige
B = 603 cranberry
C = 605 vy lt cranberry
D = 726 golden yellow
E = 816 garnet

Needles

No. 10 sharp needle
No. 9 straw (milliner's) needle
No. 22 chenille needle

Supplies

No. 30 gauge uncovered wire
Piece of calico or plain fabric for working petals
Fine tweezers

Order of work

Use the chenille needle for sinking the wires, the straw needle for the French knots and the sharp needle for all other embroidery.

Transfer the outlines of the petals, column and throat to the calico.

Petals

Cut five pieces of uncovered wire, each 12cm (4¾") long.

Bend and shape each length of wire into a petal shape *(see diag., bottom left)*. Using the sharp needle, couch each piece to the calico.

Overcast the centre vein and then work blanket stitch around the edge of each petal. Fill in the petals with long and short stitch. Carefully cut around the edges, taking care not to cut any of the stitching.

Column

Cut an 11cm (4⅜") length of wire. Bend it to the column shape, leaving two tails of wire extending. Work the column and cut it out in a similar manner to the petals.

Throat

Cut a 15cm (6") length of wire. Bend and shape it to fit the throat template, leaving two tails of wire extending. Couch in place. Cover the wire using blanket stitch as before. Fill in the throat with long and short stitch, fanning the stitches from the centre outwards.

Work two rows of satin stitch along the centre of the throat. Stitch the French knots around the outer edge and between the two rows of satin stitch.

Cut out the throat in the same manner as the petals.

Assembling the orchid

Using a pair of tweezers, gently curl each of the five petals to form the orchid shape. Repeat for the column and the throat, turning the lower edge of the throat frill outwards.

Using the chenille needle, insert each of the petals into the fabric. Repeat for the column and then the throat. Trim the wire to 1cm (⅜") and secure with couching stitches.

Reshape the petals, column and frill of the throat until the desired look is achieved.

Embroidery key

All embroidery is worked with one strand of thread.

Petals

Central vein = B (couching, overcast stitch)

Petal outlines = C (couching, blanket stitch)

Inside of petals = B and C (long and short stitch)

Column

Outline = A (couching, blanket stitch)

Inside of column = A and B

(long and short stitch)

Throat

Outline = A (couching, blanket stitch)

Inside of throat = A (long and short stitch)

Central veins = D (satin stitch)

Spots on frill = E (French knot, 2 wraps)

PANSY

Viola tricolor by Heather Scott

This design uses
Long and short stitch, Satin stitch,
Split stitch, Stem stitch, Straight stitch

Requirements

Threads

DMC stranded cotton
A = blanc
B = 340 med blue-violet
C = 341 lt blue-violet
D = 806 dk peacock blue
E = 814 vy dk garnet
F = 869 vy dk hazelnut brown
G = 3047 lt yellow-beige
H = 3051 dk green-grey
I = 3052 med green-grey
J = 3747 vy lt blue-violet
K = 3807 cornflower blue
Anchor stranded cotton
L = 186 lt aquamarine
M = 259 vy lt pine green
N = 1030 hyacinth

Needle

No. 10 sharp needle

Thou canst not stir a flower / Without
troubling of a star.   *Francis Thompson*

...Pansies, that's for thoughts.
William Shakespeare

Order of work

Flowers

Embroider the petals in satin stitch. Overlay the centre of the lower petal on the left pansy with straight stitches to achieve a two tone effect. Add straight stitches along the edge of the lower petal on the centre pansy to achieve a similar effect.

Stitch the petal markings with straight stitches of varying lengths. Fill the centres with satin stitch and then work 1–2 straight stitches on each side of the centre, forming an inverted 'V'.

Buds

Work the petals in satin stitch and then the calyxes.

Stems and leaves

Using the darker green thread, stitch the main stem in satin stitch and the finer stems in stem stitch. Add the small leaves and then stitch the two large leaves.

Butterfly

Using the darker thread, completely cover the wings in satin stitch. Change thread and stitch the lighter sections of the wings over the previous stitching.

Stitch the body with straight stitches. Work two stitches in the opposite direction to create the head. For each antennae, work a long straight stitch and add a tiny straight stitch across the tip.

Embroidery key

All embroidery is worked with one strand of thread unless otherwise specified.

Large flower

Upper petals = K (satin stitch)

Middle petals = C (satin stitch)

Lower petal = G (satin stitch), B (straight stitch)

Petal markings = E (straight stitch)

Centre = M (satin stitch), A (2 strands, straight stitch)

Left flower

Upper petals = N (satin stitch)

Middle petals = J (satin stitch)

Lower petal = J (satin stitch), G (straight stitch)

Petal markings = E (straight stitch)

Centre = M (satin stitch), A (2 strands, straight stitch)

Right flower

Upper petals = K (satin stitch)

Middle petals = B (satin stitch)

Lower petal = G (satin stitch)

Petal markings = E (straight stitch)

Centre = M (satin stitch), A (2 strands, straight stitch)

Large bud

Petals = B and K (satin stitch)

Calyx = H and I (satin stitch)

Small bud

Petals = B (satin stitch)

Calyx = I (satin stitch)

Stems and leaves

Main stem = H (satin stitch)

Small stems = H (stem stitch)

Large leaves = I (satin stitch)

Small leaves = H (split stitch)

Butterfly

Body and head = F (2 strands, straight stitch)

Antennae = F (2 strands, straight stitch)

Wings = D and L (satin stitch)

I send thee pansies while the year is young, Yellow as sunshine, purple as the night; Flowers of remembrance, ever fondly sung / By all the chiefest of the Sons of Light; And if in recollection lives regret

For wasted days, and dreams that were not true, I tell thee that the 'pansy freak'd with jet' / Is still the heart's-ease that the poets knew / Take all the sweetness of a gift unsought,

And for the pansies send me back a thought

Sarah Dowdney

PANSY

Viola tricolor by Jane Nicholas

This design uses

Beading, Blanket stitch, Couching, Detached chain, French knot, Granitos, Long and short blanket stitch, Padded satin stitch, Stem stitch, Straight stitch

Requirements

Threads & beads

DMC stranded cotton
A = 310 black
B = 741 med tangerine
C = 744 lt yellow
D = 745 vy lt yellow
E = 783 med topaz
F = 793 med cornflower blue
G = 3347 med yellow-green
Madeira stranded silk
H = 0113 egg yolk
I = 0114 lt pumpkin
Au Ver à Soie, Soie d'Alger
J = 1336 vy dk grape
K = 3322 lt silver purple
L = 3323 med silver purple
M = 3336 vy dk purple
Machine silk stitch 50
N = 24 deep purple
Kreinik metallic 1 ply cord
O = 105C antique silver
Mill Hill glass seed beads
P = 00128 yellow

Mill Hill frosted glass beads
Q = 60168 sapphire
R = 62034 blue-violet

Needles

No. 10 straw (milliner's) needle
No. 10 crewel needle
No. 18 chenille needle

Supplies

2 pieces of quilter's muslin
Fine florist's wire
Clear nylon thread
Fine tweezers

Order of work

Use the straw needle for attaching the beads and the crewel needle for all thread embroidery. The chenille needle is used for sinking the wires.

Forget-me-nots

Using the nylon thread and 3–4 stitches, attach a yellow bead for the centre of each flower. Ensure the hole is facing upwards. Attach five blue beads around each centre. Use the pale beads on one flower and the darker beads on the other flower. Secure one bead for the largest bud.

Work the stem in stem stitch and then the detached chain leaves. Stitch the green buds, using two strands of thread for the first bud and one strand for the remaining two buds.

Finally add a French knot in the centre of the yellow beads.

Bee

Embroider a granitos of seven straight stitches for the body padding.

Cover the padding with satin stitch stripes, working two stitches for each stripe. Work a French knot for the head and two detached chains for the wings.

Pansies

Place one piece of muslin in a hoop and transfer the petal outlines. Cut the wire into 12cm (4¾") lengths.
Using tweezers, bend and shape one length of wire into a petal shape. Leave one tail of wire.

Couch the wire to the muslin. Using the same thread, work blanket stitch to cover the wire. Work a row of close long and short blanket stitches around the outer third of the petal just inside the edge. Fill the remainder of the petal with straight stitches, keeping the stitch direction towards the base of the petal.

Embroider the remaining petals in the same manner, leaving two tails of wire on petal 5. Work straight stitches of varying lengths for the markings on the middle and lower petals.

Cut out each petal, taking care not to cut the stitching and the tails of wire. Attach the petals to the fabric in numerical order. Take the wires through the same hole in the fabric, one at a time. Secure the tails with tiny stitches on the back of the fabric and trim.

Stitch a French knot for the centre. Shape the petals with the tweezers until you achieve the desired effect.

Work the second flower in the same manner, adding the purple spot to the lower petal.

Embroidery key

All embroidery is worked with one strand of thread unless otherwise specified.

Left pansy

Upper petals = L (couching, blanket stitch, long and short blanket stitch), K (straight stitch)

Middle petals = D (couching, blanket stitch), C (long and short blanket stitch, straight stitch)

Lower petal = H (couching, blanket stitch, long and short blanket stitch), B and I (straight stitch)

Petal markings = N (straight stitch)

Centre = B (6 strands, French knot, 1 wrap)

Right pansy

Upper petals = M (couching, blanket stitch, long and short blanket stitch), J (straight stitch)

Middle petals = L (couching, blanket stitch, long and short blanket stitch), K (straight stitch)

Lower petal = H (couching, blanket stitch, long and short blanket stitch), M (couching, blanket stitch), B and I (straight stitch)

Petal markings = N (straight stitch)

Centre = B (6 strands, French knot, 1 wrap)

Forget-me-nots

Petals = F and Q, or R (beading)

Centres = P (beading), H (French knot, 2 wraps)

Large bud = F and R (beading)

Small buds = G (1–2 strands, French knot, 1 wrap)

Stem = G (stem stitch)

Leaves = G (2 strands, detached chain)

Bee

Body = A (granitos), A and E (padded satin stitch)

Head = A (French knot, 2 wraps)

Wings = O (detached chain)

PANSY

Viola by Joan Gibson

This design uses

Blanket stitch, Detached chain, French knot, Straight stitch

Requirements

Threads

DMC stranded cotton

A = 310 black
B = 327 vy dk lavender
C = 522 fern green
D = 743 yellow
E = 3743 vy lt antique violet

Needle

No. 10 crewel needle

Order of work

Each pansy flower is stitched in exactly the same way. Beginning on the right hand side, work the upper petal first. Change thread and continue around the circle for the lower petals. Work a detached chain on each side of the flower, overlapping the joins of the two colours. Ensure these stitches are slightly longer than the blanket stitches.

Embroider a straight stitch in the centre of each detached chain and then work straight stitches of varying lengths over the lower petals. Add a yellow French knot to the centre.

Scatter detached chain leaves around the edges of the design.

Embroidery key

All embroidery is worked with one strand of thread.

Flowers

Upper petals = B (blanket stitch)

Lower petals = E (blanket stitch)

Middle petals = E (detached chain)

Petal markings = A (straight stitch)

Centres = D (French knot, 2 wraps)

Leaves = C (detached chain)

PANSY

Viola x wittrockiana by Carol Hawkins

This design uses
Encroaching stem stitch, Long and short stitch,
Satin stitch, Stem stitch, Straight stitch

Requirements

Threads

DMC stranded cotton
A = 743 yellow
B = 745 vy lt yellow
C = 746 off-white
D = 972 deep canary
E = 3053 green-grey
F = 3371 black-brown
G = 3685 wine
H = 3731 vy dk dusky rose
I = 3733 dusky rose
J = 3803 lt wine
Gumnut Yarns 'Stars' stranded silk
K = 628 dk eucalypt
L = 629 vy dk eucalypt
M = 589 vy dk apple green
N = 829 vy dk peach melba
Madeira stranded silk
O = 0112 custard
P = 0811 vy dk shell pink
Q = 0812 dk shell pink
R = 1407 avocado green
S = 2208 lt old gold

Needle

No. 10 sharp needle

Take all the sweetness of a gift unsought, And for the
pansies send me back a thought. *Sarah Dowdney*

Order of work

Use the photograph as a guide to thread colour changes within the design.

Foliage

Beginning at the base, work the main stems in encroaching stem stitch, gradually tapering into stem stitch for the upper sections. Add the leaves in satin stitch. Work the stems for the buds in stem stitch.

Flowers

Starting at the outer edge and working towards the centre, embroider the two upper petals of each flower in long and short stitch. Work the lower petal next, followed by the two side petals.

Stitch the centre of each flower face with vertical satin stitches.

Embroider radiating straight stitches on the lower and side petals for markings.

Work 2–3 straight stitches on each side of the centre forming an inverted 'V'.

Buds

Embroider the petals in satin stitch, then work the calyxes with straight stitches of varying lengths.

Embroidery key

All embroidery is worked with one strand of thread.

Flower 1

Upper petals = G and H (long and short stitch)

Middle petals = Q and S (long and short stitch)

Lower petal = A, D, P and Q (long and short stitch)

Petal markings = F (straight stitch)

Centre = E (satin stitch), C (straight stitch)

Flower 2

Upper petals = B and C (long and short stitch)

Middle petals = B and S (long and short stitch)

Lower petal = B, D and S (long and short stitch)

Petal markings = P (straight stitch)

Centre = E (satin stitch), C (straight stitch)

Flower 3

Upper petals = P, Q and S (long and short stitch)

Middle petals = Q and S (long and short stitch)

Lower petal = A, O and P (long and short stitch)

Petal markings = F (straight stitch)

Centre = E (satin stitch), C (straight stitch)

Flower 4

Upper petals = G, H and J (long and short stitch)

Middle petals = H and I (long and short stitch)

Lower petal = A, I, J and N (long and short stitch)

Petal markings = F (straight stitch)

Centre = E (satin stitch), C (straight stitch)

Flower 5

Upper petals = G, J and O (long and short stitch)

Middle petals = O and S (long and short stitch)

Lower petal = A, O, P and S (long and short stitch)

Petal markings = F (straight stitch)

Centre = E (satin stitch), C (straight stitch)

Small buds

Petal = G (satin stitch)

Calyx = L (straight stitch)

Large bud

Petals = H and J (satin stitch)

Calyx = K (straight stitch)

Foliage

Leaves = K, L, M and R (satin stitch)

Stems = K, L and R (encroaching stem stitch, stem stitch)

Pansy is an English way of saying the French word 'pansée' which means thought. *The Language of Flowers*

PANSY
Viola tricolor by Carolyn Pearce

This design uses
Back stitch, Blanket stitch, Colonial knot, Fly stitch, Long and short stitch,
Split stitch, Split back stitch, Straight stitch

Requirements

Threads

Appletons 2 ply crewel wool
A = 101 vy lt purple
B = 102 lt purple

Gumnut Yarns 'Daisies' 1 ply wool
C = 232 vy lt pansy
D = 233 lt pansy
E = 237 dk pansy
F = 646 dk khaki
G = 743 vy lt daffodil
H = 744 lt daffodil

YLI silk floss
I = 23 purple
J = 24 Imperial purple

Minnamurra stranded cotton
K = 110 purple/gold

Stef Francis 'Silk Impressions' 12 ply silk
L = 009 variegated wisteria

Kacoonda 2 ply silk
M = 306 vy dk olive

Kacoonda thick silk
N = 105 Victorian autumn

Madeira stranded silk
O = 1714 pewter grey

Needles

No. 5 crewel needle
No. 10 crewel needle
No. 22 chenille needle

Supplies

Cream felt
Fusible appliqué paper

Order of work

Use the chenille needle for working
the centre, the no. 5 crewel needle
when stitching with the wools and
2 ply silk and the no. 10 crewel needle
for all other thread embroidery.

Flower

Fuse the appliqué paper to the felt and
cut out the petals. Position the first
petal on the fabric and secure with
stab stitches. Following the diagram,
attach the remaining petals, one at
a time, in the same manner *(see diag.,
bottom left)*. Attach two pieces of felt for
petals 2 and 5, placing the larger piece
over the smaller one.

Using the lighter yarn, edge petal 1
with long and short blanket stitch and
work a row of split stitch. Change
thread colour and fill the remainder of
the petal in split stitch. Work the
remaining petals in the same manner.
On the lower petal, work the dark
pansy coloured section first.

Embroider straight stitches of
varying lengths over the petals
for markings. Begin these stitches near
the centre and fan them across
the petals.

Add a colonial knot for the centre
and work back stitch between the
petals. Pull these stitches firmly so they
define each one.

Leaves

Following the step-by-step instructions
on page 49, stitch the leaves, making
every third fly stitch longer than the
previous two. Outline the leaf in split
back stitch.

Embroidery key

All embroidery is worked with one strand of thread.

Flower

Upper petals = A (long and short blanket stitch, split stitch), B (split stitch)

Upper petal markings = I and L (straight stitch)

Middle petals = C (long and short blanket stitch, split stitch), D (split stitch)

Lower petal = E (blanket stitch), G (long and short blanket stitch, split stitch), H (split stitch)

Markings on middle and lower petals = J and K (straight stitch)

Between petals = O (back stitch)

Centre = N (colonial knot)

Leaves = F and M (fly stitch, split back stitch)

A thing of beauty is a joy for ever. *John Keats*

PANSY

Viola tricolor by Di Kirchner

This design uses

Blanket stitch, Detached chain, French knot, Granitos, Stem stitch, Straight stitch

Requirements

Threads

DMC stranded cotton
A = 327 vy dk lavender
B = 743 yellow
C = 3346 hunter green

Needle

No. 9 crewel needle

Order of work

Flower

Beginning from the same point on the fabric and using the lavender thread, work two overlapping detached chains on each side for the upper petals. Change to the yellow thread and stitch nine detached chains. Embroider five straight stitches of varying lengths over the yellow petals for markings. Ensure the stitches radiate from the same point at the centre of the flower. Add a French knot to the centre.

Bud

Stitch a granitos of three straight stitches for the petals of each bud. Work two detached chains around the base of each bud for sepals.

Stems and leaves

Work the stems in stem stitch. Embroider the leaves with blanket stitches which all radiate from the same point on the fabric.

Embroidery key

All embroidery is worked with two strands of thread unless otherwise specified.

Flower

Upper petals = A (detached chain)

Middle and lower petals = B (detached chain)

Petal markings = A (1 strand, straight stitch)

Centre = B (French knot, 1 wrap)

Buds

Petals = A (granitos)

Sepals = C (1 strand, detached chain)

Stems = C (1 strand, stem stitch)

Leaves = C (1 strand, blanket stitch)

POPPY

Papaver orientale by Jane Nicholas

This design uses

Blanket stitch, Chain stitch, Couching, Detached back stitch, Ghiordes knot, Straight stitch, Long and short blanket stitch

Requirements

Threads

DMC stranded cotton
A = 666 bright Christmas red
B = 3346 hunter green
C = 3801 vy dk melon
DMC no. 8 perlé cotton
D = 902 maroon
Au Ver à Soie, Soie d'Alger
E = 3326 vy dk purple
F = 4636 dk plum

Needles

No. 7 crewel needle
No. 10 crewel needle
No. 9 straw (milliner's) needle
No. 18 chenille needle
No. 26 tapestry needle

Supplies

Mill Hill pebble bead
No. 5202 amethyst
75cm (29½") fine florist's wire
Piece of quilter's muslin
Eyebrow comb
Fine tweezers

Order of work

The leaves are stitched on the base fabric and the petals of the poppy are made separately. Use the no. 7 crewel needle when stitching with the perlé cotton and the tapestry needle when working the detached back stitch. The chenille needle is used for sinking the wires of the petals and the no. 10 crewel needle is used for all other embroidery.

Leaves

Work the central vein of the leaves in chain stitch. Pad the surface of the leaves with straight stitch. Starting at the base of the leaf and working to the tip, work long and short blanket stitch along each side of the centre vein, angling the stitches as you work.

Flower

Mount the muslin in a hoop and transfer the petal outlines. Cut the florist's wire into 12cm (4¾") lengths. Using tweezers, bend and shape each length of wire into a petal shape, leaving two tails.

Couch one wire to the muslin. Using the same thread, work blanket stitch to cover the wire. Work a row of close long and short blanket stitches around the outer third of the petal just inside the edge.

Change thread colour and work the centre of the petal in long and short stitch. Change to the darkest colour and work the petal marking in long and short stitch.

Embroider the remaining petals in the same manner. Cut out each petal, taking care not to cut the stitching and the tails of wire.

Attach the petals and work the centre following the step-by-step instructions on the opposite page.

Embroidery key

All embroidery is worked with one strand of thread unless otherwise specified.

Flower

Petal outlines = C (couching, blanket stitch)

Petals = C (long and short blanket stitch), A (long and short stitch)

Petal markings = E (long and short stitch)

Centre = D and F (detached back stitch)

Stamens = E (2 strands, Ghiordes knot)

Leaves

Leaf veins = B (chain stitch)

Padding = B (straight stitch)

Leaves = B (long and short blanket stitch)

Poppy – The symbol of remembrance.

STEP-BY-STEP ASSEMBLING THE POPPY

1 **Attaching the bead.** With the hole facing up, stitch the pebble bead to the centre of the leaves with four stitches.

2 **Attaching the petals.** Using the chenille needle, sink each tail through a separate hole in fabric close to bead. Attach opposite petal in same manner.

3 Repeat for the remaining petals, placing one petal and then its opposite.

4 Bend the wire behind each petal on the back of the fabric and secure with tiny stitches. Trim excess wire.

5 **Centre.** Work eight evenly spaced straight stitch spokes over the bead, extending each spoke approx 2mm (⅛") into a petal.

6 Secure the thread on the back of the fabric. Beginning at the centre, begin to work a detached back stitch over each spoke.

7 Continue until the bead is completely covered.

8 **Stamens.** Work sixteen ghiordes knots around the centre. Stitch a knot at the end of each spoke and one in between.

9 Cut all the loops and trim the threads to approx 6mm (¼").

10 Comb the knots with the eyebrow comb until they are fluffy. Retrim to approx 3mm (⅛").

11 **Finishing.** Using the tweezers, bend the petals so they curl to the desired shape.

Completed poppy.

POPPY

Papaver rhoeas by Joan Gibson

This design uses
Blanket stitch, French knot, Satin stitch,
Stem stitch, Straight stitch

Requirements

Threads

DMC stranded cotton
A = 310 black
B = 350 med coral
C = 368 lt pistachio green

Needle
No. 10 crewel needle

Order of work

Flowers

Embroider a blanket stitch pinwheel for the facing bloom and a partial blanket stitch pinwheel for the side view bloom. The remaining flower is stitched in two sections. Stitch the section closest to the stem first. Begin the second section at the upper right hand corner of the first. Fill the centres with closely packed French knots.

Foliage

Work the stems in stem stitch and then the small bud in satin stitch.

Begin each leaf at the base. Work stem stitch along the centre, making the last stitch longer than the previous stitches. Add pairs of straight stitches along the stem stitch, angling them towards the tip of the leaf.

Embroidery key

All embroidery is worked with one strand of thread.

Flowers

Petals = B (blanket stitch)

Centres = A (French knot, 2 wraps)

Bud = C (satin stitch)

Stems = C (stem stitch)

Leaves = C (stem stitch, straight stitch)

PETUNIA

Petunia x hybrida by Di Kirchner

This design uses
Blanket stitch, Detached chain,
French knot, Stem stitch

Requirements

Threads

DMC stranded cotton
A = 745 vy lt yellow
B = 3346 hunter green
C = 3746 dk blue-violet

Needle
No. 9 crewel needle

Order of work

Embroider a blanket stitch pinwheel for the petals of each flower. Add single French knots for the centres.

Work the stems in stem stitch and then the detached chain leaves.

Embroidery key

All embroidery is worked with two strands of thread unless otherwise specified.

Flowers

Petals = C
(blanket stitch)

Centres = A (1 strand,
French knot, 1 wrap)

Stems = B
(stem stitch)

Leaves = B
(detached chain)

PRIMULA

Primula veris by Heather Scott

This design uses

Blanket stitch, French knot, Long and short stitch,
Satin stitch, Stem stitch, Straight stitch

Embroidery key

All embroidery is worked with one strand of thread unless otherwise specified.

Flowers

Petals of upper flowers = H (blanket stitch),
D (long and short stitch)

Petals of lower flower = G (blanket stitch), D and
H (long and short stitch)

Centres = C (straight stitch), A (2 strands,
French knot, 1 wrap)

Calyxes = F and G (satin stitch)

Buds

Petals = H (satin stitch)

Calyxes = F (long and short stitch)

Stems and leaves

Stems = F (stem stitch)

Large leaves = B and F (satin stitch)

Small leaves = E and F (straight stitch)

Requirements

Threads

DMC stranded cotton
A = 444 dk lemon
B = 471 vy lt avocado green
C = 472 ultra lt avocado green
D = 961 dk dusky rose
E = 3052 med green-grey
F = 3347 med yellow-green
G = 3713 vy lt salmon
H = 3716 vy lt dusky rose

Needle

No. 10 sharp needle

Order of work

Flowers

Stitch the petals from the outer edge towards the centre. Work a star of straight stitches in the centre. For each point of the star, work 4–6 straight stitches which share the same hole at the tip but fan out at the base. Add a French knot to the middle.

Stitch the bud petals and pink section of the flower calyxes in satin stitch. Work the bud calyxes in long and short stitch and the green sections of the flower calyxes in satin stitch.

Stems and leaves

Embroider the large leaves in satin stitch, completing each section before beginning the next. Take care that the stitches of one section do not intrude into another section.

Work the stems in stem stitch and then add a mass of overlapping straight stitches to the base of the plant for the small leaves.

PRIMULA

Primula auricula by Susan O'Connor

This design uses

Back stitch, Blanket stitch, Cross stitch, French knot, Long and short stitch,
Padded satin stitch, Satin stitch, Stem stitch, Straight stitch

And in green underwood and cover / Blossom by blossom the spring begins.   *A.C. Swinburne*

Requirements

Threads

Madeira stranded silk

A = 0806 dk antique violet
B = 0807 antique violet
C = 0811 vy dk shell pink
D = 0812 dk shell pink
E = 1409 vy lt avocado green
F = 1510 lt Jacobean green
G = 1603 lt khaki green
H = 1701 vy lt blue-green
I = 2207 vy lt old gold
J = 2211 topaz

Needle

No. 12 sharp needle

Order of work

Use the photograph as a guide to thread colour changes within the design.

Violet flowers

Stitch the petals of the side view flowers and buds, beginning at the outer edge and working towards the base.

Embroider the petals of the facing flower in a similar manner, adding a round of pale gold stitches near the centre. Work a circle of pale green satin stitches to begin the centre of the facing flower. Fill the remaining space with old gold satin stitches in one direction for padding. Cover the padding with a second layer of satin stitches in the opposite direction. Partially outline the centre in back stitch.

Red flowers

Stitch the petals of the facing flowers from the outer edge towards the centre. Embroider the centres in the same manner as the centre of the facing violet flower.

Work the calyx of the side view flower in the upper group. Using the darkest thread, begin stitching the petals of the side view flowers. Change to the lighter thread to complete the flowers. Take 2–3 long and short stitches over the calyx of the side view flower in the upper group of flowers.

Foliage

Complete one section of a leaf at a time. Work the narrower sections in blanket stitch, changing to satin stitch in the places where the edge of the leaf goes behind another section of the design. Begin the wider sections with blanket stitch and then fill in the remainder with long and short stitch. Embroider the stems with satin stitch.

Border

First, stitch the violet sections in satin stitch and then the pink sections, followed by the green. Using the topaz thread, work a straight stitch between each pink and green section and then a cross stitch which covers the violet and pink sections. Add a French knot at the centre of the cross. Outline both edges of the border with stem stitch.

Embroidery key

All embroidery is worked with one strand of thread.

Violet flowers

Petals of facing flower = B (blanket stitch), A and I (long and short stitch)

Centre = G (satin stitch), I (padded satin stitch)

Centre outline = A (back stitch)

Petals of side view flowers = A (blanket stitch), B (blanket stitch, long and short stitch)

Buds = A and B (blanket stitch, long and short stitch)

Red flowers

Petals of facing flowers = C (blanket stitch, long and short stitch), J (satin stitch)

Centres = G (satin stitch), I (padded satin stitch)

Centre outlines = A (back stitch)

Petals of side view flowers = C (blanket stitch), D (blanket stitch, long and short stitch)

Calyx of upper side view flower = G (satin stitch)

Leaves = E (blanket stitch, long and short stitch), F and G (blanket stitch, long and short stitch, satin stitch), H (blanket stitch, satin stitch)

Stems = E, F and G (satin stitch)

Border

Filling = A, D and G (satin stitch), J (straight stitch)

Crosses = J (cross stitch, French knot, 1 wrap)

Outlines = J (stem stitch)

The garden: 'a place of mysterious sweet scents, a paradise of forbidden fruits, a dreamland of splendid colour.' *Marion Cran*

PRIMULA

Primula veris by Joan Gibson

This design uses

Blanket stitch, Bullion loop, Couching, French knot, Stem stitch, Straight stitch

Requirements

Threads

DMC stranded cotton
A = 725 dk golden yellow
B = 727 lt golden yellow
C = 3347 med yellow-green

Needles

No. 9 crewel needle
No. 10 straw (milliner's) needle

Order of work

Flowers

Work five bullion loops around the centre circle for the petals.

Couch each loop at the outer edge with a tiny straight stitch. Using the darker yellow thread, work a single straight stitch inside each bullion loop. Fill the centre of each flower with a single French knot.

Stems and leaves

Embroider the leaves in blanket stitch, keeping the stitches very close together. Work the stems in stem stitch.

Embroidery key

All embroidery is worked with one strand of thread unless otherwise specified.

Flowers

Petals = B (5 bullion loops, 24 wraps, couching), A (2 strands, straight stitch)

Centres = A (2 strands, French knot, 1 wrap)

Stems = C (stem stitch)

Leaves = C (blanket stitch)

Genus Primulaceae

There are approximately 400 spieces of the genus primulaceae. They live in a wide range of habitats, from wet boggy soils and marshland through to Alpine areas.

They are spread widely throughout the Northern Hemisphere and nearly half of the species are from the Himalayas. There are however, a few species found in the Southern Hemisphere.

A book is like a garden carried in the pocket. *Chinese proverb*

QUEEN ANNE'S LACE

Anthriscus sylvestris by Kris Richards

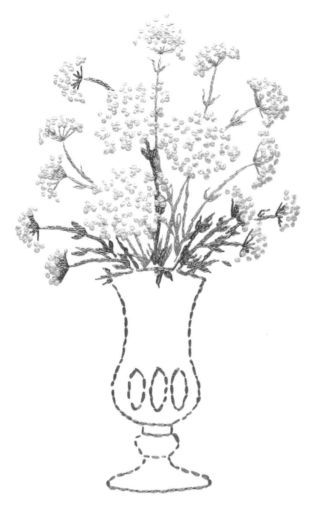

Requirements

Threads

DMC stranded cotton
A = blanc
B = 341 lt blue-violet
C = 3013 lt khaki green
Madeira stranded silk
D = 1408 lt avocado green

Needles

No. 9 crewel needle
No. 7 crewel needle

Order of work

Embroider all the stems and leaves
first. Stitch clusters of French knots
at the ends of the small stems and
three large clusters in the centre of
the arrangement.

Outline the vase in back stitch.

Embroidery key

*All embroidery is worked with one strand
of thread unless otherwise specified.*

Flowers = A (2 strands, French knot,
2 wraps)

Stems

Main stems = C or D (stem stitch)

Small flower stems = C or D (straight stitch)

Leaves = C or D (detached chain)

Vase = B (3 strands, back stitch)

This design uses

Back stitch, Detached chain, French knot, Stem stitch, Straight stitch

> Flowers have an expression of countenance as much as men or animals.
> Some seem to smile, some have a sad expression, some are pensive
> and diffident, others again are plain, honest and upright.
>
> Henry Ward Beecher

ROSE

Rosa eglanteria by Heather Scott

This design uses

Back stitch, French knot, Satin stitch,
Stem stitch, Straight stitch

It takes a long time to grow an old friend.   *John Leonard*

Requirements

Threads

DMC stranded cotton
A = blanc
B = 727 lt golden yellow
C = 733 med olive green
D = 818 baby pink
E = 3348 lt yellow-green
F = 3713 vy lt salmon
G = 3733 dusky rose
H = 3772 dk mocha
I = 3819 chartreuse
Anchor stranded cotton
J = 681 Jacobean green

Needles

No. 10 sharp needle
No. 9 crewel needle

Love Planted a Rose

Love planted a rose, and the
world turned sweet, where the
wheatfield blows, love planted
a rose.

Up the mill-wheel's prose
ran a music beat.

Love planted a rose, and the
world turned sweet.

Katherine Lee Bates

Order of work

Use the crewel needle when stitching
with two strands of thread and the
sharp needle for all other embroidery.

Flowers

Embroider the petals of the flowers and
bud in satin stitch. Using the darkest
pink thread, work several tiny straight
stitches along the edges of the petals
and longer straight stitches between
the petals.

Fill the centre of the facing flower
with satin stitch. Work straight stitch
stamens over the centre and add a
French knot to the end of each one.

Foliage

Work the satin stitch leaves and sepals.
Stitch the main stem with three rows of
stem stitch. Add a horizontal straight
stitch across the bottom.

Embroider the remaining stems in
stem stitch. Work tiny straight stitches
for the thorns.

Dragonfly

Stitch the wing outlines and veins in
back stitch. Add angled white straight
stitches along the veins.

Embroider the head and body in
satin stitch and then work two straight
stitches for the antennae.

...there is no place more pleasant
than a garden. *William Coles*

Embroidery key

*All embroidery is worked with one strand
of thread unless otherwise specified.*

Flowers

Petals = F (satin stitch)

Petal markings = G (straight stitch)

Centre of facing flower = I (satin stitch)

Stamens of facing flower = B (straight stitch,
French knot, 1 wrap)

Sepals of side view flower = C (satin stitch)

Buds

Petals of large bud = D (satin stitch)

Sepals = C and J (satin stitch)

Foliage

Main stem = J (stem stitch, straight stitch)

Small stems = C and J (stem stitch)

Thorns = J (straight stitch)

Leaves = C or E (satin stitch)

Leaf veins = J (back stitch, stem stitch)

Dragonfly

Body and head = H (2 strands, satin stitch)

Wings = H (2 strands, back stitch),
A (straight stitch)

Antennae = H (2 strands, straight stitch)

ROSE

Rosa by Kris Richards

Requirements

Threads

DMC stranded cotton
A = 899 med rose
B = 3011 dk khaki green
C = 3350 ultra dk dusky rose
D = 3713 vy lt salmon

Needles

No. 1 straw (milliner's) needle
No. 8 crewel needle

This design uses
Bullion knot, Fly stitch, Stem stitch

Roses for health

During the Second World War, rosehip syrup was found to have a very high Vitamin C content and was commonly given to babies.

Roses – A Guide to Cultivation
by Janet Browne

And the rose herself has got / Perfume which on earth is not.   *John Keats*

Order of work

Use the straw needle for the bullion knots and the crewel needle for all other embroidery.

Roses

Embroider the large roses following the step-by-step instructions on the opposite page. The lower left rose has one extra outer petal.

Beginning with the darkest pink, work a single bullion knot for the centre of each small rose. Change to the mid pink thread and stitch two bullion knots around the centre of the upper small rose. Surround the centre of the remaining small rose with three bullion knots. Change to the lightest pink thread and stitch three bullion knots around the lower section of each rose.

Embroider the sepals of the upper rose with four bullion knots and those of the lower rose with two bullion knots.

Rosebuds

Work one bullion knot for the petals of the lower rosebud and two for the upper rosebud. To form the sepals of each bud, stitch two bullion knots around the petals and surround these with a fly stitch.

Stems and leaves

Stitch the fly stitch leaves following the step-by-step instructions on page 49. Add the stem stitch stems.

Embroidery key

All embroidery is worked with four strands of thread unless otherwise specified.

Large roses

Centre = C (2 bullion knots, 6 wraps)
Inner petals = A (3 bullion knots, 10 wraps)
Outer petals = D (6–7 bullion knots, 12 wraps)

Small roses

Centres = C (bullion knot, 6 wraps)
Inner petals = A (2–3 bullion knots, 10 wraps)
Outer petals = D (3 bullion knots, 12 wraps)
Sepals = B (2–4 bullion knots, 10 wraps)

Rosebuds

Petals = A (1–2 bullion knots, 10 wraps)
Sepals = B (2 bullion knots, 10 wraps), B (1 strand, fly stitch)

Stems = B (1 strand, stem stitch)
Leaves = B (1 strand, fly stitch)

STEP-BY-STEP LARGE BULLION ROSE

1 **Centre.** Using the darkest pink thread, stitch two bullion knots side by side.

2 **Inner petals.** Surround the centre with three bullion knots which slightly overlap each other.

3 **Outer petals.** Beginning on the right hand side, work four overlapping bullion knots around the sides and bottom of the inner petals.

4 Work two bullion knots below the previous petals. For the lower left rose, add an additional bullion knot below the previous two.

83

ROSE

Rosa eglanteria by Margo Fanning

Requirements

Threads

Appletons 2 ply crewel wool
A = 242 lt olive green
B = 243 olive green
C = 311 ultra lt brown olive
D = 752 vy lt rose pink
E = 991 white
Paterna Persian Yarn
F = D511 dk verdigris
Kacoonda hand dyed medium embroidery wool
G = 108 variegated rose

Needle

No. 24 chenille needle

Order of work

Use the photograph as a guide to yarn colours within the design.

Flower

Stitch the petals from the outer edge towards the centre. Embroider the first row in closely worked blanket stitch and the remaining rows in long and short stitch. When stitching the folded sections, work the blanket stitch so the 'purls' are towards the centre.

For the centre, work three green French knots and surround these with a mass of brown olive French knots.

Buds

Embroider the petals of the three buds in satin stitch. Add a granitos calyx to the base of each bud.

Foliage

Work the stems in rope stitch and then the leaves in satin stitch. Place straight stitches over the leaves to achieve the variegated look. Add leaf veins to all the leaves except the two smallest leaves on the lower stem and the leaf to the left of the lowest bud.

Work overlapping straight stitches over the buds for the new foliage.

This design uses

Back stitch, Blanket stitch, French knot, Granitos, Long and short stitch, Rope stitch, Satin stitch, Straight stitch

More exquisite than any other is the autumn rose.   *Theodore D'Aubigne*

Embroidery key

All embroidery is worked with one strand of yarn unless otherwise specified.

Flower
Petals = G (blanket stitch), D and E (long and short stitch)
Centre = B and C (French knot, 1 wrap)

Buds
Petals = G (satin stitch)
Calyxes = A (2 strands, granitos), B blended with F (1 strand of each, granitos)
New foliage = A (straight stitch), B blended with F (1 strand of each, straight stitch)

Stems and leaves
Stems = F (rope stitch)
Leaves = A, B and F (satin stitch, straight stitch)
Leaf veins = A or F (back stitch)

ROSE

Rosa by Di Kirchner

This design uses

Bullion knot, Detached chain,
Straight stitch

Requirements

Threads

DMC stranded cotton
A = 520 dk fern green
B = 742 lt tangerine
C = 743 yellow
D = 745 vy lt yellow

Needles

No. 9 crewel needle
No. 9 straw (milliner's) needle

Embroidery key

All embroidery is worked with one strand of thread unless otherwise specified.

Flowers

Centres = B (2 strands, 2 bullion knots,
6–8 wraps)

Inner petals = C (2 strands, 3 bullion knots,
10 wraps)

Outer petals = D (2 strands, 5 bullion knots,
12 wraps)

Bud

Petals = C (2 strands, 2 bullion knots, 9 wraps)

Sepals = A (detached chain, straight stitch)

Stems = A (straight stitch)

Leaves = A (detached chain, straight stitch)

Order of work

Use the straw needle for the bullion
knots and the crewel needle for all
other embroidery.

Flowers

Using the darkest yellow thread, stitch
two bullion knots side by side for the
centre of each rose. Surround the
centre on the left with three bullion
knots for the inner petals and then
work five bullion knots around these
for the outer petals. For the flower on
the right, partially surround the centre
with three inner petals. Work the five
outer petals below the inner petals.

Bud

Stitch two bullion knots side by side for
the petals. Beginning at the base of
the bud, add a detached chain on each
side for the sepals. Work two straight
stitches from the tip of the bud for the
remainder of the sepals.

Stems and leaves

Use long straight stitches for the stems.
Work the flower stems first and then
the leaf stems. Ensure the two lower
leaf stems cross the flower stems to
help hold them in place.

Finally stitch the leaves, working
a detached chain with a straight stitch
inside for each leaf.

Perfumed roses

Rose perfume and rose water, which is made from
steeping perfumed petals in boiling water, have been
used for over 2,000 years. Traditionally various
solvents and pure alcohol were used to extract the
fragrance from the petals of highly perfumed roses.
Today various chemicals, blended together, are used to
create synthetic rose perfumes. Real roses, however,
are used to produce more composite floral fragrances.

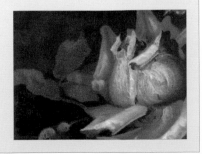

ROSE

Rosa by Carolyn Pearce

This design uses
Colonial knot, Fly stitch,
Gathering, Rolling, Smocker's knot

Requirements

Threads & ribbons

Kacoonda fine silk
A = 107 soft autumn green
YLI 601 fine metallic thread
B = 7 iced green
The Thread Gatherer Silk 'n Colors stranded silk
C = SNC 027 maidenhair fern
Kacoonda hand dyed silk ribbon 7mm (⁵⁄₁₆") wide
D = 6C autumn rose
Kacoonda hand dyed silk ribbon 13mm (½") wide
E = 302 peace
Colour Streams hand dyed silk ribbon 13mm (½") wide
F = 18 antique ivory
Vintage Ribbons hand dyed silk ribbon 13mm (½") wide
G = blush

Needles

No. 10 crewel needle
No. 10 straw (milliner's) needle
No. 12 sharp needle
No. 18 chenille needle

Supplies

Fine machine sewing thread to match 13mm (½") ribbons

Order of work

Use the crewel needle for stitching the leaves and the chenille needle for stitching the centre of the rose. The sharp needle is used for gathering and attaching the petals and the straw needle for rolling the ribbon.

Flower

Following the step-by-step instructions on the opposite page, make ten ribbon petals.

Work a very loose colonial knot for the centre. Using matching machine sewing thread, work a stab stitch through the centre of the colonial knot and then stitch the inner petals around it. Position the first petal so the roll is away from the knot and secure it with a stab stitch at each end. Position the second petal in the same manner as the first, overlapping the two petals. Repeat for the third petal.

Secure the four middle petals in the same manner. Attach the outer petals so the roll faces inwards. Use the eye of the chenille needle to push any tails of thread underneath the petals and work more stab stitches to ensure they are all secure.

Leaves

Stitch the leaves following the step-by-step instructions on page 49, adding a smocker's knot to the base of each one. Use the photograph as a guide to thread colour.

Cabbage Rose – Ambassador of Love. *The Language of Flowers*

Embroidery key

All thread embroidery is worked with one strand.

Flower

Centre = D (colonial knot)

Inner petals = F (3 rolled and gathered petals)

Middle petals = G (4 rolled and gathered petals)

Outer petals = E (3 rolled and gathered petals)

Leaves = A, B and C (fly stitch, smocker's knot)

STEP-BY-STEP ROSE PETAL

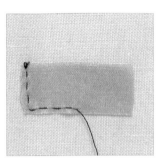

1 Cut a 26mm (1") length of ribbon. Using a knotted thread, work tiny running stitches along left end and approx. halfway along lower edge. Leave thread dangling.

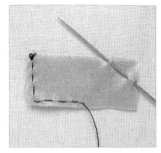

2 Pin the straw needle diagonally across the top right corner.

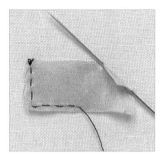

3 Fold the corner of the ribbon over the needle.

4 Roll the ribbon tightly until the needle lines up with both ends of the running stitch.

5 Pick up the dangling thread. Take a stitch through the roll.

6 Remove the straw needle. Pull up the running stitches so the petal cups slightly.

7 Secure the thread with two back stitches and cut off the excess.

8 Carefully trim tail of ribbon near back stitches and trim any whiskers of ribbon or thread. The petal is now ready to be attached to the fabric.

SNOWDROP

Galanthus nivalis by Angela Dower

Requirements

Threads & ribbons

Au Ver à Soie, Soie d'Alger
A = 3723 med pistachio green
YLI silk floss
B = 157 drab olive
C = 500 white
**Kacoonda hand dyed silk ribbon
4mm (³⁄₁₆″) wide**
D = no. 8E lt olive
**Glen Lorin hand dyed silk ribbon
2mm (⅛″) wide**
E = green sands
YLI silk ribbon 4mm (³⁄₁₆″) wide
F = 3 white

Needles

No. 20 tapestry needle
No. 18 chenille needle
No. 22 chenille needle
No. 8 straw (milliner's) needle

Supplies

Green fine tipped fabric marker
Lace pins
Small piece of plastic

This design uses
Couching, French knot, Ribbon stitch, Side ribbon stitch, Straight stitch,
Twisted detached chain, Whipped chain stitch, Whipped stem stitch

Flowers leave a part of their fragrance in the hands that bestow them.   *Chinese proverb*

Order of work

Use the straw needle for all thread embroidery, the no. 22 chenille needle for the 2mm (⅛") ribbon, the no. 18 chenille needle for the 4mm (³⁄₁₆") ribbon and the tapestry needle for all whipping.

Stems

Following the step-by-step instructions which begin below, stitch the three flower stems and then the stem for the bud.

Flowers

Embroider the upper right flower following the step-by-step instructions.

Work the flower on the left hand side in a similar manner but work the middle stitch in each layer of petals before working the side petals. Using the fabric marker, add a dot to the tip of the middle petal in the upper layer.

Stitch the lower right flower following steps 1–10 of the step-by-step instructions. Add a green dot to the middle petal before completing it. Embroider the three petals of the upper layer with ribbon stitches. Fold the ribbon before completing the ribbon stitch for the two petals on the right. Couch the upper petals in place.

Bud

Work a twisted detached chain in the white ribbon. Cover this with a straight stitch, ensuring the ribbon is untwisted. Stitch the calyx in the same manner as those on the flowers.

Leaves

Embroider all the leaves with ribbon stitch. Take the ribbon for the two middle leaves behind the stems. Add a twist to the ribbon of the vertical leaves and a fold in the ribbon of the bent leaves. Couch the bent leaves at the folds to hold their shape.

Embroidery key

All thread embroidery is worked with one strand.

Stems

Lower stems = A (whipped chain stitch)

Hoods = D (ribbon stitch)

Upper stems = B (whipped stem stitch)

Flowers

Petals = F (side ribbon stitch, ribbon stitch), C (couching)

Calyxes = D (French knot, 1 wrap, straight stitch)

Bud

Petals = F (twisted detached chain, straight stitch)

Calyx = D (French knot, 1 wrap, straight stitch)

Leaves = E (ribbon stitch), B (couching)

STEP-BY-STEP SNOWDROP

1 Mark the position of the stem and the entry and exit points for the ribbon on the right side of the fabric.

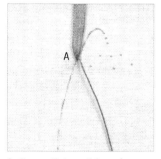

2 **Stem.** Bring ribbon for hood to front at A and lay it away from lower stem. Bring thread for lower stem to front inside fold of the ribbon and close to A.

3 Work chain stitch to the base of the stem.

4 Using the same thread in the tapestry needle, whip up the chain stitches.

Who loves a garden loves a greenhouse too.   *William Cowper*

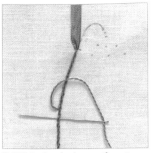

5 Whip back down the stem over the previous whipping.

6 Fold the ribbon out flat and hold in place with lace pins. Using a new thread, work the remainder of the stem in stem stitch.

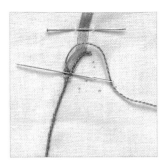

7 Using the same thread in the tapestry needle, whip back along the stem stitch.

8 Finish thread. Remove pins. Finish hood as a ribbon stitch. This will fold the ribbon over the stem stitch creating the hooded effect.

9 **Petals.** Bring ribbon to front at base of petal. Lay out flat to the right. Place plastic beneath it. Dot ribbon with green fabric marker.

10 Wait a few moments and then complete a side ribbon stitch. Work a petal to the left in the same manner.

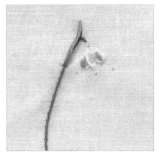

11 Work a ribbon stitch for the centre petal.

12 Begin a second layer of petals working side ribbon stitches for the outer ones.

13 Work a ribbon stitch for the centre petal.

14 **Calyx.** Change ribbon. Work a French knot at the base of the petals.

15 Work a short straight stitch from end of stem to base of petals. Spread ribbon so it covers French knot. Gently pull ribbon all the way through.

16 **Finishing.** Using the white thread, couch the sides of the outer petals to hold their shape.

SALVIA

Salvia patens by Joan Gibson

This design uses
Couching, Detached chain,
French knot, Straight stitch

Requirements

Threads

DMC stranded cotton
A = 792 dk cornflower blue
B = 3347 med yellow-green

Needle

No. 10 crewel needle

Order of work
Work a long straight stitch for each
stem and couch it in place at
approximately 4mm (³⁄₁₆") intervals.
Using the same thread, scatter French
knots around the upper half of
each stem.
    Stitch the clump of detached chain
leaves from the outer edge inwards.

Embroidery key

*All embroidery is worked with one strand
of thread.*

Flowers = A (French knot, 2 wraps)
Stems = A (straight stitch, couching)
Leaves = B (detached chain)

STATICE

Limonium sinuatum by Di Kirchner

This design uses
French knot, Stem stitch, Straight stitch

Requirements

Threads

DMC stranded cotton
A = 743 yellow
B = 3013 lt khaki green

Needle

No. 9 crewel needle

Order of work
Embroider seven clusters of French
knots for the flowers.
    Stitch the stems in stem stitch. Add
tiny straight stitches along the stems
for leaves and several straight stitches
at the top of each stem to link
the flowers.

Embroidery key

*All embroidery is worked with two strands
of thread.*

Flowers = A (French knot, 1 wrap)
Foliage
Main stems = B (stem stitch)
Flower stems = B (straight stitch)
Leaves = B (straight stitch)

SUNFLOWER

Helianthus x multiflorus by Di Kirchner

Requirements

Threads

DMC stranded cotton
A = 743 yellow
B = 840 med beige
C = 3021 vy dk Jacobean green
D = 3346 hunter green

Needle

No. 9 sharp needle

Order of work

Stitch the petals with detached chains worked very closely together. Using blended threads, fill the centre with closely packed French knots.

Embroider the stem in stem stitch and then the leaves in satin stitch. Complete one half before beginning the next and keep the stitches angled towards the tip of the leaf.

Embroidery key

All embroidery is worked with two strands of thread.

Flower

Petals = A (detached chain)

Centre = B blended with C (1 strand of each, French knot, 1 wrap)

Stem = D (stem stitch)

Leaves = D (satin stitch)

This design uses

Detached chain, French knot, Satin stitch, Stem stitch

The versatile sunflower

By far one of the tallest flowers in the garden, the sunflower is not only a handsome flower – with its brilliant yellow petals and dark brown/black centre – but is also a source of food. Every part of the plant is used in some form.

The leaves and stalks are used for fodder, making cloth and even as a substitute for tobacco. The seeds can be eaten and made into oil and soap.

When the oil is cold pressed it is a great salad oil and is also used for cooking and for the making of margarine.

A flowerless room is a soulless room... *Vita Sackville-West*

SUNFLOWER

Helianthus x multiflorus by Joan Gibson

This design uses

Fly stitch, French knot, Stem stitch, Straight stitch, Whipped stem stitch

Requirements

Threads

DMC stranded cotton
A = 471 vy lt avocado green
B = 743 yellow
C = 841 lt beige
D = 3363 med pine green

Needles

No. 7 crewel needle
No. 9 crewel needle
No. 24 tapestry needle

Order of work

Use the no. 7 crewel needle for the flower petals and the tapestry needle for the whipping. The no. 9 crewel needle is used for all other embroidery.

Flower

Each petal is created with three straight stitches that are worked in and out of the same holes in the fabric. Stitch a petal along each marked line.

Fill the inner circle of the centre with tightly packed green French knots.

Using the beige thread, fill the remainder of the centre with French knots packed closely together.

Stems

Embroider the main stem and then the three leaf stems in stem stitch.

Whip the main stem, taking the needle under every stem stitch.

Leaves

Work the fly stitch leaves following the step-by-step instructions on page 49. Finish the base of each leaf with 2–3 straight stitches.

No, the heart that has truly lov'd never forgets, But as truly loves on to the close, As the sunflower turns on her god, when he sets, The same look which she turn'd when he rose! *Thomas Moore*

Embroidery key

All embroidery is worked with one strand of thread unless otherwise specified.

Flower	Stems
Petals = B (3 strands, straight stitch)	Main stem = D (whipped stem stitch)
Centre = A (2 strands, French knot, 1 wrap), C (2 strands, French knot, 2 wraps)	Leaf stems = D (stem stitch)
	Leaves = D (fly stitch, straight stitch)

SWEET PEA

Lathyrus odoratus by Joan Gibson

This design uses
Back stitch, Double back stitch

Embroidery key

All embroidery is worked with one strand of thread.

Stems and tendrils = C (back stitch)

Large flower

Dark petal = D (back stitch, double back stitch)

Light petal = B (double back stitch)

White petal = A (double back stitch)

Side view flower

Dark petal = D (back stitch, double back stitch)

Light petal = B (double back stitch, back stitch)

Calyx = C (double back stitch)

Bud

Petals = D (double back stitch)

Petal markings = D (back stitch)

Calyx = C (double back stitch)

Life is a flower of which love is the honey. **Victor Hugo**

Requirements

Threads

DMC stranded cotton

A = blanc

B = 963 ultra lt dusky rose

C = 3052 med green-grey

D = 3716 vy lt dusky rose

Needle

No. 10 crewel needle

Order of work

Stems, tendrils and calyxes

Embroider the main stem, stopping and starting at the edges of the large flower. Work the tendrils next. Stitch the shadow worked calyxes, beginning at the positions indicated on the design.

Large flower

Shadow embroider the white petal first. Start the lighter petal with back stitch along the section indicated on the pattern and then change to double back stitch to fill the petal. Work the remaining petal in the same manner.

Side view flower

Stitch the lighter petal first, beginning on the lower edge. Work the darker petal from its tip towards the lighter petal, finishing with back stitch along the edge shared with the lighter petal.

Bud

Work the petal markings in back stitch. Begin the petal with back stitch along the lower left hand side and then change to double back stitch to fill the petal.

SWEET PEA

Lathyrus odoratus by Terry Loewen

Requirements

Threads

DMC stranded cotton
A = 209 lavender
B = 211 lt lavender
C = 340 med blue-violet
D = 341 lt blue-violet
E = 368 lt pistachio green
F = 743 yellow
G = 744 lt yellow
H = 3607 fuchsia
I = 3608 lt fuchsia

Needle

No. 9 crewel needle

Order of work

Foliage

Using stem stitch, embroider the stems, tendrils and outlines of the leaves and sepals. Fill the leaves and sepals with the same thread colour.

Flowers

Each flower is worked in a similar manner. On one flower, outline the upper edge of the lower petal in stem stitch. Fill the petal with a combination of long and short stitch and satin stitch, covering the stem stitch outline. Use long and short stitch in the larger areas and satin stitch in the smaller areas.

Outline the upper edge of the next petal in stem stitch and fill with satin stitch. If the flower has a third petal, stitch this in the same manner as the second petal.

Embroider the remaining flowers in the same way.

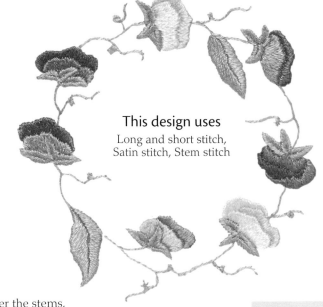

This design uses
Long and short stitch,
Satin stitch, Stem stitch

Delicate Pleasures, Inspirations 26

Embroidery key

All embroidery is worked with one strand of thread.

Lavender flower

Lower petal = B
(stem stitch, long and short stitch, satin stitch)

Second petal = A
(stem stitch, satin stitch)

Blue flowers

Lower petals = D
(stem stitch, long and short stitch, satin stitch)

Second petals = C
(stem stitch, satin stitch)

Yellow flowers

Lower petals = G
(stem stitch, long and short stitch, satin stitch)

Second petals = F
(stem stitch, satin stitch)

Third petal = G (stem stitch, satin stitch)

Pink flowers

Lower petals = I
(stem stitch, long and short stitch, satin stitch)

Second petals = H
(stem stitch, satin stitch)

Third petal = I (stem stitch, satin stitch)

Stems and tendrils = E
(stem stitch)

Sepals

Outlines = E (stem stitch)

Filling = E (satin stitch)

Leaves

Outlines = E (stem stitch)

Filling = E (long and short stitch, satin stitch)

THISTLE

Onopordum nervosum by Jane Nicholas

This design uses
Blanket stitch, Chain stitch,
Ghiordes knot, Lattice couching,
Padded satin stitch, Satin stitch,
Split back stitch, Straight stitch

We blossom under praise like flowers in sun and dew; We open, we reach, we grow.   *Gerhard E. Frost*

Requirements

Threads

DMC stranded cotton
A = 356 med terra cotta
B = 520 dk fern green
C = 522 fern green
D = 3041 med antique violet
E = 3042 lt antique violet
F = 3740 dk antique violet

Needles

No. 9 straw (milliner's) needle
No. 6 crewel needle
No. 10 crewel needle

Supplies

Cream felt
Fusible webbing
Eyebrow comb

Order of work

Use the straw needle for the ghiordes knots, the no. 6 crewel needle when stitching with three strands of thread and the no. 10 crewel needle for all other embroidery.

Stems and leaf veins

Stitch the main stem in chain stitch. Begin the leaf stems at the main stem with two strands of thread. Remove one strand when approximately three quarters of the way along the leaf vein and continue to the end with one strand.

Leaves

Outline the leaf with split back stitch. Fill the shapes with straight stitches, parallel to the leaf vein, for padding. Working one half at a time, cover both the padding and the outline with satin stitch. Embroider the spikes with a straight stitch from each leaf point.

Thistle base

Fuse the webbing to the felt and cut out the three shapes for the base. Secure the smallest shape to the fabric with stab stitches. Cover with the medium sized shape and secure with stab stitches. Repeat for the largest shape.

Embroider blanket stitch around the entire outer edge. Cover the felt with satin stitch. Work lattice couching over the satin stitch.

Thistle head

Beginning with the darkest colour, work ghiordes knots in the spaces between the peaks of the base. Work a second row of knots. Change to the next darkest blend of threads and work two more rows. Continue in this manner, grading the thread colour from dark to light.

Trim the loops to approximately 1cm (⅜") long. Comb the pile with the eyebrow comb. Continue trimming and combing until the pile is fluffy and the desired length.

A Scottish Thistle, Inspirations 22

Embroidery key

All embroidery is worked with one strand of thread unless otherwise specified.

Thistle head = D, D blended with E, D blended with F, E and F (2 strands, ghiordes knot)

Thistle base

Outline = C (blanket stitch)

Filling = C (satin stitch)

Markings = A and B (lattice couching)

Main stem = B (3 strands, chain stitch)

Leaves

Veins and stems = B (1–2 strands, chain stitch)

Outlines = B (split back stitch)

Filling = B (padded satin stitch)

Spikes = B (straight stitch)

Just living is not enough... One must have sunshine, freedom and a little flower.   *Hans Christian Andersen*

TULIP

Tulipa by Susan O'Connor

This design uses
Blanket stitch, Long and short stitch, Satin stitch, Split stitch, Straight stitch

Requirements

Threads

Madeira stranded silk
A = 0401 dk terra cotta
B = 0402 terra cotta
C = 0403 lt terra cotta
D = 0803 lavender
E = 0815 vy lt shell pink
F = 1312 hunter green
G = 1407 avocado green
H = 1408 lt avocado green
I = 1409 vy lt avocado green
J = 1508 olive green
K = 1603 lt khaki green
L = 2213 dk topaz

Needle
No. 12 sharp needle

Order of work

Use the photograph as a guide to thread colour changes within the design.

Flowers and foliage

Embroider the flowers and foliage following the step-by-step instructions on the opposite page and on page 100. Omit the split stitch outline from the foremost petal of the lowest flower.

When working the leaves, stitch leaves 3 and 5 first, followed by leaf 2 and then leaves 1 and 4.

Border

Stitch the topaz segments first. Change to the lavender thread and fill in the spaces. Outline each side of the border with split stitch.

Embroidery key

All embroidery is worked with one strand of thread.

Flowers

Petals = A and B (blanket stitch, long and short stitch), C (blanket stitch, long and short stitch, split stitch)

Highlights = E (straight stitch)

Leaves

Leaf 1 = G (satin stitch), H (blanket stitch, satin stitch), I (blanket stitch) Leaf 2 = J (blanket stitch, long and short stitch)

Leaf 3 = H (blanket stitch), K (blanket stitch, long and short stitch)

Leaf 4 = G (blanket stitch), J (blanket stitch, satin stitch)

Leaf 5 = H (blanket stitch), I (blanket stitch, long and short stitch)

Stems

Stems = F (blanket stitch, split stitch), G (blanket stitch)

Highlights = H (straight stitch)

Border

Filling = D and L (satin stitch)

Outline = G (split stitch)

...Fires gardens with a joyful blaze
Of tulips, in the morning's rays.

Ralph Waldo Emerson

The Tulip – The Queen of all Bulbous flowers.   *The Treasury of Tulips*

STEP-BY-STEP TULIP

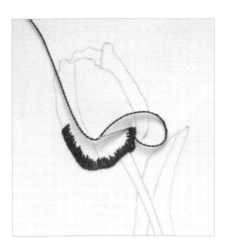

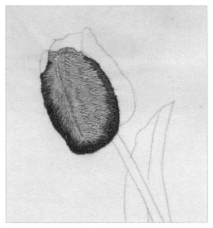

1 Trace the design onto the fabric and place it in a hoop. Using the darkest thread, work blanket stitch around the lower edge of the foremost petal.

2 Change to the next shade of thread. Work blanket stitch along the sides and long and short stitch along the previous stitching. Take long and short stitches into previous stitching.

3 Change to the next shade of thread. Work blanket stitch around the tip and fill the remainder of the petal with long and short stitch.

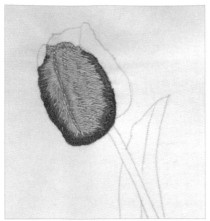

4 Using the same thread, work split stitch along the centre of the petal.

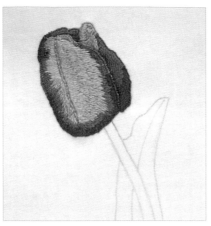

5 Work the remaining petals in the same manner, omitting the split stitch.

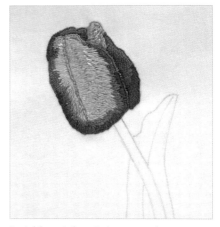

6 Add straight stitches over the previous stitching for highlights. These stitches follow the same direction as the previous ones.

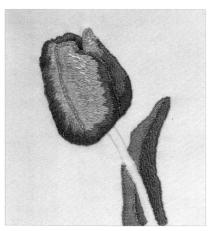

7 **Leaf.** Stitch the leaf from the outer edges towards the centre. Complete one half before beginning the next.

8 **Stem.** Using the darkest green, work blanket stitches, keeping the 'purls' on the left side of the stem. Work split stitch along the opposite edge.

9 Change thread. Work blanket stitch over the first layer of stitches, keeping the 'purls' next to the split stitch. Add straight stitch highlights, keeping the stitches at the same angle as the previous ones.

Ladies like variegated tulips, show; 'Tis to their changes half their charms they owe...   *Alexander Pope*

TULIP

Tulipa by Di Kirchner

This design uses

Detached chain, Stem stitch, Straight stitch

Requirements

Threads

DMC stranded cotton
A = 666 bright Christmas red
B = 726 golden yellow
C = 987 forest green

Needle

No. 9 crewel needle

Order of work

Stitch three detached chains for the petals of each flower. Begin each stitch at the same position on the fabric and fan them slightly. Place a straight stitch inside each one. Embroider the stems and leaves in stem stitch.

Embroidery key

All embroidery is worked with two strands of thread.

Flowers = A or B (detached chain, straight stitch)
Stems = C (stem stitch)
Leaves = C (stem stitch)

TULIP

Tulipa by Joan Gibson

This design uses

Satin chain, Stem stitch, Straight stitch

Requirements

Threads

DMC stranded cotton
A = 347 vy dk salmon
B = 368 lt pistachio green

Needle

No. 9 crewel needle

Order of work

Embroider two vertical satin stitches at the centre of a flower, then work two slightly shorter stitches on each side. Finish with a straight stitch over the top of the previous centre stitch.

Stitch each stem with a single line of stem stitch. Work two lines of stem stitch, side by side, for the leaves. Add the tip of the bent leaf on the left hand side with a single line of stem stitch.

Embroidery key

All embroidery is worked with one strand of thread unless otherwise specified.

Flowers = A (2 strands, satin stitch, straight stitch)
Stems = B (stem stitch)
Leaves = B (stem stitch)

The cottage garden; most for use design'd, Yet not of beauty destitute. ***Charlotte Smith***

VIOLET

Viola odorata by Angela Dower

Requirements

Threads & ribbons

Madeira stranded silk
A = 1603 lt green-grey
Rajmahal stranded rayon
B = 93 chardonnay
C = 144 persimmon
YLI silk floss
D = 24 Imperial purple
Glen Lorin hand dyed silk ribbon 2mm (⅛") wide
E = rippon
Colour Streams hand dyed silk ribbon 4mm (³⁄₁₆") wide
F = 21 purple genie

Needles

No. 20 chenille needle
No. 22 chenille needle
No. 9 crewel needle
No. 9 straw (milliner's) needle

This design uses

Couching, French knot, Long and short stitch, Raised stem stitch, Ribbon stitch, Stem stitch, Straight stitch, Twisted detached chain, Whipped back stitch

A violet in the youth of primy nature,
Forward, not permanent, sweet, not lasting,
The perfume and suppliance of a minute;
No more.   *William Shakespeare*

Order of work

Use the no. 20 chenille needle for the 4mm (³⁄₁₆″) ribbon and the no. 22 chenille needle with the 2mm (¹⁄₈″) ribbon. Work the French knots with the straw needle and all other thread embroidery with the crewel needle.

Stems and leaves

Fill the two halves of the large leaf with long and short stitch for padding. Work the stitches parallel to the centre vein. Stitch a framework of straight stitches on each half of the leaf *(see diag., below)*. Work raised stem stitch across the framework until each half of the leaf is completely covered. Stitch the vein in stem stitch.

Embroider the stems in back stitch, working two rows of back stitch side by side for the segment below the junction of the large leaf's stem. Using the same thread, whip the stems. Add two ribbon stitch leaves to the junction on the lowest stem.

Flowers

Stitch 5–6 petals for each of the mature blooms. Using blended threads, add a French knot to the centre of each one.

Buds

Stitch a twisted detached chain and overlay it with a straight stitch for the petals of the small bud.

Form the larger buds with three overlapping straight stitches for the drooping petals and a ribbon stitch for the upturned petal. Couch the petals in place.

Work two overlapping ribbon stitches for the sepals on each bud. Add a tiny ribbon stitch to the end of the stem on the upper flower for the calyx.

Embroidery key

All thread embroidery is worked with one strand unless otherwise specified.

Flowers

Petals = F (straight stitch)

Centre = B blended with C (1 strand of each, French knot, 1 wrap)

Calyx = E (ribbon stitch) or none

Large buds

Petals = F (straight stitch, ribbon stitch), D (couching)

Sepals = E (ribbon stitch)

Small bud

Petals = F (twisted detached chain, straight stitch)

Sepals = E (ribbon stitch)

Stems and leaves

Stems = A (whipped back stitch)

Large leaf padding = A (long and short stitch)

Large leaf = A (raised stem stitch)

Large leaf vein = A (stem stitch)

Small leaves = E (ribbon stitch)

Floral flavours

The culinary use of flowers can be dated back to 140BC. Violets, like many other flowers, are edible.

They can be crystallised and used as cake decorations, as well as being used to flavour salads and desserts.

One of the worst mistakes you can make as a gardener is to think you're in charge. *Janet Gillespie*

VIOLET

Viola odorata by Carol Hawkins

This design uses
Encroaching stem stitch, Long and short stitch, Satin stitch, Stem stitch, Straight stitch

Requirements

Threads

DMC stranded cotton
A = 550 vy dk violet
B = 552 med violet
C = 553 violet
D = 554 lt violet
Gumnut Yarns 'Stars' stranded silk
E = 549 dk forest green
F = 589 dk apple green
Madeira stranded silk
G = 1408 avocado green
H = 2209 old gold
I = 2401 soft white

Needle

No. 10 sharp needle

Order of work

Use the photograph as a guide to thread colour changes within the design.

Leaves and stems

Beginning at the base, work the three main stems in satin stitch and encroaching stem stitch. Gradually taper to stem stitch for the upper sections.

Add the leaves in satin stitch and the leaf buds in stem and satin stitch. Work the shorter stems and the stems for the bud and leaves in encroaching stem stitch and stem stitch.

I know a bank whereon the wild thyme blows, where oxlips and the nodding violet grows… *William Shakespeare*

Flowers

All the flowers are worked in a similar manner.

Beginning at the outer edge and working towards the centre, embroider each petal in long and short stitch. Gradually change from the lightest shade to the darkest or the darkest to the lightest as you work. Overlay some of the petals with straight stitches.

Using the old gold thread, stitch 2–3 straight stitches for the centre. Surround this with straight stitch highlights in the white thread.

VIOLET

Viola odorata by Joan Gibson

This design uses
Blanket stitch, Detached chain, French knot, Stem stitch

Requirements

Threads

DMC stranded cotton
A = 327 vy dk lavender
B = 522 fern green
C = 725 dk golden yellow

Needle

No. 10 crewel needle

Order of work

Leaves and stems

Work the leaves in blanket stitch, radiating all the stitches from the same point. Stitch curved lines of stem stitch for the stems.

Flowers

Embroider two detached chains for the upper petals of the mature flowers and three for the lower petals. Leave a small space in the centre. Fill the space with a yellow French knot. Create the bud with two drooping detached chains.

VIOLET

Viola odorata by Carolyn Pearce

This design uses

Colonial knot, Fly stitch, Granitos, Straight stitch

Requirements

Threads

DMC stranded cotton
A = 3721 dk shell pink
B = 3834 dark grape
Madeira stranded silk
C = 1603 lt green-grey
Rajmahal stranded rayon
D = 45 baby camel
YLI silk floss
E = 000 white
Stef Francis Silk Impressions 12 ply silk
F = 009 field of violets

Needle

No. 9 crewel needle

Order of work

Flower

Each petal is a granitos of five straight stitches. Work the two upper petals so they just touch each other. Stitch the lower petals on each side and then the one in the centre, making this petal slightly longer than the others. Work a fly stitch, with a long anchoring stitch, around the end of each petal and a straight stitch over the outer half. Embroider tiny white straight stitches, radiating from the centre, on the three lower petals. Using blended threads, add a cluster of three colonial knots to the centre.

Leaves

Stitch three pairs of fly stitches around the flower. Keep the 'arms' of the fly stitches uneven and the anchoring stitch long.

Violet sorbet

1 egg white
2 tablespoons of lime juice
50g (23oz) caster sugar
200ml (½ cup) sugar syrup
4 tablespoons of Créme de Violette

Put the egg white and caster sugar to one side, mix the rest of the ingredients together and freeze until mushy.

Beat the egg white and fold in the caster sugar. Add all the mixture together and freeze.

Serve topped with a few fresh violet flowers.

The Lover's Book of Days

Embroidery key

All embroidery is worked with one strand of thread unless otherwise specified.

Flower

Petals = F (granitos)

Petal tips = B (fly stitch)

Petal markings = B and E (straight stitch)

Centre = 1 strand of A blended with 2 strands of D (3 strands, colonial knot)

Leaves = C (fly stitch)

...Gardens are not made, by singing: –
'Oh, how beautiful!' and sitting in
the shade... *Rudyard Kipling*

WATTLE

Acacia pycnantha by Joan Gibson

This design uses
French knot, Granitos, Stem stitch, Straight stitch

Requirements

Threads

DMC stranded cotton
A = 725 dk golden yellow
B = 3347 med yellow-green

Needles

No. 9 crewel needle
No. 6 crewel needle

Order of work

Use the no. 6 crewel needle for the French knots and the no. 9 crewel needle for all remaining embroidery.

Foliage

Using stem stitch, work the main stems and then the leaf stems.

Begin each leaf at the tip with two straight stitches, which run along the middle of the leaf. Work an angled straight stitch from one side to the middle, and then a stitch from the other side to the middle. Continue working the the stitches close together and alternating from side to side until reaching the base of the leaf. Embroider the small leaves at the tip of the longest stem with granitos of 2–4 straight stitches.

Flowers

Work large French knots in loosely packed clusters.

Embroidery key

All embroidery is worked with two strands of thread unless otherwise specified.

Flowers = A (6 strands, French knot, 1 wrap)

Foliage
Main stems = B (stem stitch)
Leaf stems = B (stem stitch)
Large leaves = B (straight stitch)
Small leaves = B (granitos)

WATTLE

Acacia baileyana by Kathryn Trippett

This design uses
French knot, Satin stitch, Stem stitch

Deep in their roots, all flowers keep the light. *Theodore Roethke*

Requirements

Threads

DMC stranded cotton
A = blanc
B = 320 med pistachio green
C = 610 vy dk taupe
D = 612 med taupe
E = 726 golden yellow

Needle

No. 9 sharp needle

Order of work

Fill the top third of one circle using A blended with E. Fill the middle third using E and the lower third using D blended with E.

Allow the knots from one third to wander into the adjacent third a little, so distinct lines do not form. Repeat for the remaining circles.

Work the three segments of stem in stem stitch. Embroider the leaves with satin stitches that run along the length of the leaves.

Embroidery key

All embroidery is worked with three strands of thread unless otherwise specified.

Flowers = A blended with E, E, and D blended with E (2 strands, French knot, 1 wrap)

Stem = C (stem stitch)

Leaves = B (satin stitch)

Encore, Inspirations 16

Gardens for health

Modern scientific research shows that sounds, colours and aromas of nature each have a unique frequency or vibration which, entering our brains, affects us emotionally, mentally and even physiologically.

With this in mind, we may begin to pro-actively choose for our garden those colours, aromas and sounds that will positively enhance our health and attitudes.

The Garden Sanctuary

WISTERIA
Wisteria sinensis by Kris Richards

Requirements

Threads

DMC stranded cotton
A = 208 dk lavender
B = 211 lt lavender
C = 554 lt violet
D = 732 olive green
E = 842 vy lt beige
F = 926 med grey-green

Needles

No. 8 crewel needle
No. 8 straw (milliner's) needle

Order of work

Use the straw needle for the French knots and the crewel needle for all other embroidery.

Stitch the outlines of the gate in back stitch.

Embroider the stems with several lines of stem stitch worked closely together.

Beginning with the darker shade of lavender, work French knots in the upper section of each raceme of wisteria. Change to the violet thread and work the middle sections. Place the occasional French knot among the darker ones to mingle the colours slightly. Change to the lighter shade of lavender and complete the lower sections. Again, place the occasional French knot among the violet ones to mingle the colours as before.

Add tiny detached chain leaves to the tops of the racemes.

This design uses
Back stitch, Granitos, French knot, Stem stitch

Embroidery key

All embroidery is worked with two strands of thread unless otherwise specified.

Flowers = A and C (French knot, 2 wraps), B (French knot, 1–2 wraps)

Stems = E (1 strand, stem stitch)

Leaves = D (detached chain)

Gate = F (back stitch)

Flowers… have a mysterious and subtle influence upon the feelings, not unlike some strains of music. They relax the tenseness of the mind. They dissolve its rigour.   *Henry Ward Beecher*

WISTERIA

Wisteria sinensis by Carolyn Pearce

Wisteria is a small genus of twining climbers. They can be trained to grow as vines, over fences or can even be grown in pots or as standards. Once mature, they burst forth with flower each year.

Wisteria sinensis, with mauve flowers, is the most commonly seen variety.

This design uses
Colonial knot, Couching, Detached chain, French knot, Ribbon stitch, Straight stitch

Requirements

Threads & ribbons
DMC stranded cotton
A = 370 med verdigris
B = 3052 med green-grey
Needle Necessities over-dyed floss
C = 178 Coventry Gardens
Kacoonda 2 ply twist silk
D = 306 vy dk olive
**Vintage Ribbon silk ribbon
4mm (³⁄₁₆") wide**
E = pine needles

Needles
No. 8 crewel needle
No. 10 crewel needle
No. 22 chenille needle

Supplies
Water-soluble fabric
Fabric stiffener
Cake decorating wire
Plastic wrap

Order of work

Use the no. 8 crewel needle for working the French and colonial knots and the no. 10 crewel needle for all other thread embroidery. Use the chenille needle for sinking the stiffened threads and working the ribbon stitch leaves.

Vine and flowers

Stitch the vine and flowers following the step-by-step instructions on the opposite page.

Leaves and stems

Stitch the stems in straight stitch. Work a detached chain leaf at the tip of each stem and two on each side. Embroider the ribbon leaves in groups of three.

Embroidery key

All thread embroidery is worked with one strand unless otherwise specified.

Flowers = C (3 strands, colonial knot, French knot, 1 wrap)

Vine and tendrils = D (laid thread), A (couching)

Leaf stems = B (straight stitch)

Leaves = B (1–2 strands, detached chain), E (ribbon stitch)

STEP-BY-STEP WISTERIA

1 **Vine.** Mix a little fabric stiffener with a few drops of water. Pull the thread through the solution, squeezing out any excess with your fingers.

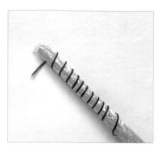

2 Cover a thick paintbrush handle or similar with plastic wrap. Wrap the thread around the handle and leave to dry.

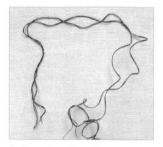

3 Uncoil and pull strands apart. Lightly twist two pieces together. Arrange the threads on the fabric and pin in place. Couch at approx 1cm (⅜") intervals.

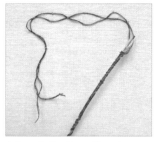

4 **Tendrils.** Restiffen the ends of the threads. Cover the wire with plastic wrap and wrap the threads around it. Let dry.

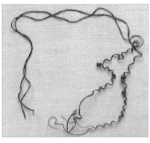

5 Uncoil the threads and arrange them on the fabric. Pin in place and couch as before.

6 Sink the ends of the vine and tendrils and secure them on the back of the fabric.

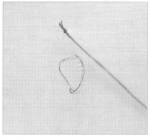

7 **Flowers.** Stretch the water-soluble fabric into a hoop. Begin with a waste knot approx 7.5cm (3") away from the design.

8 Work tightly packed colonial knots, adding the occasional French knot. Work from top to bottom and side to side so threads crisscross on the back.

9 Continue until the flowers are complete, finishing near the top. Do not cut off the tail of thread. Cut away the excess fabric.

10 Soak the flowers in cold water for a few minutes and then leave to dry.

11 Take tails of thread to back of fabric and secure. Work tiny stab stitches across top of flowers to hold them in place.

12 Work the straight stitch stems and then the leaves to complete the design.

ZINNIA

Zinnia elegans by Sharon Venhoek

This design uses
Bullion knot, Couching, Detached chain, French knot, Outline stitch

Embroidery key

*All embroidery is worked with one strand
of thread unless otherwise specified.*

Yellow flowers

Outer petals = E (8–11 bullion loops,
40 wraps, couching)

Inner petals = E (7–9 bullion loops,
25 wraps, couching)

Centre = E (French knot, 2 wraps),
D (2 strands, French knot, 2 wraps)

Orange flowers

Outer petals = A (9–10 bullion loops,
40 wraps, couching)

Inner petals = A (9–10 bullion loops,
25 wraps, couching)

Centre = A (French knot, 2 wraps),
E (2 strands, French knot, 2 wraps)

Foliage

Stems = B (2 strands, outline stitch)

Leaves = B and C (2 strands,
detached chain)

Requirements

Threads

DMC stranded cotton
A = 350 med coral
B = 520 dk fern green
C = 523 lt fern green
D = 745 vy lt yellow
E = 972 deep canary

Needle

No. 10 straw (milliner's) needle

Supplies

Painted ceramic urn

Order of work

Flowers

Each flower is stitched in the same manner. Work approximately ten bullion loops for the outer petals. Couch each petal to the fabric at its tip. Stitch the inner petals on top of the outer petals.

Couch the tips of the petals to the previous layer of bullion loops.

Using the same thread, work a French knot at the very centre. Change thread and encircle this knot with a tight cluster of yellow French knots until there is no fabric visible at the centre.

Foliage

Embroider the stems in outline stitch and then add the leaves with detached chains.

Urn

Glue the urn to the fabric so it just covers the ends of the stems.

Patterns

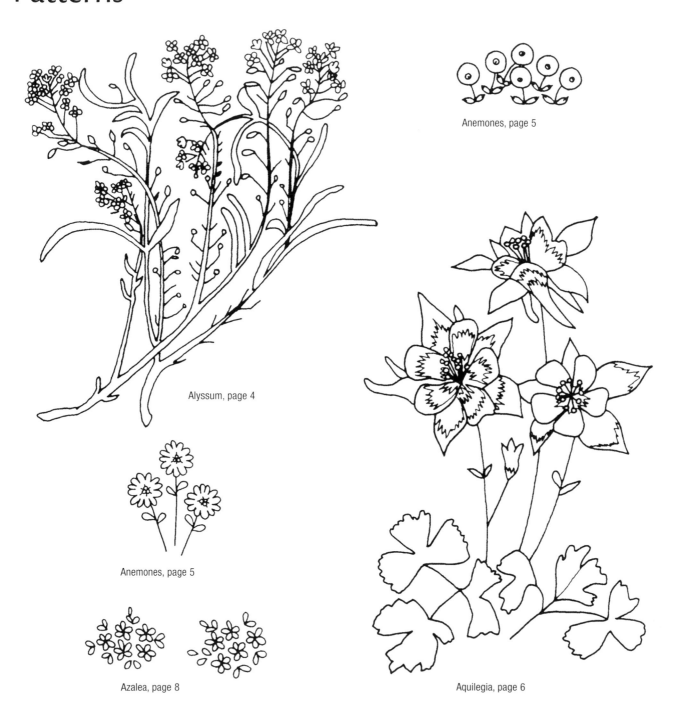

Anemones, page 5

Alyssum, page 4

Anemones, page 5

Azalea, page 8

Aquilegia, page 6

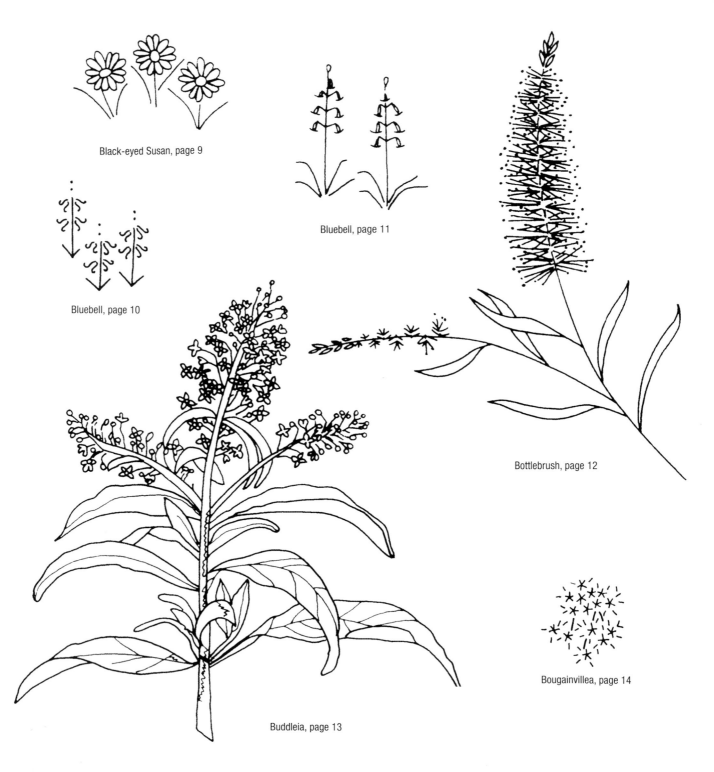

Black-eyed Susan, page 9

Bluebell, page 11

Bluebell, page 10

Bottlebrush, page 12

Bougainvillea, page 14

Buddleia, page 13

Camellia, page 14

Carnation, page 16

Clivia, page 17

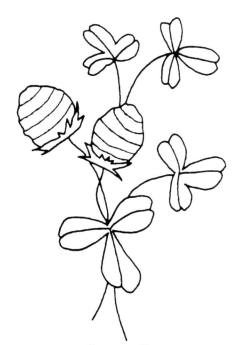

Clover, page 16

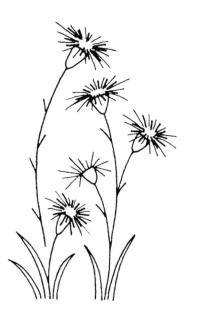

Cornflower, page 18

Daffodil, page 20

Daffodil, page 21

Crocus, page 19

Cyclamen, page 19

Dahlia, page 24

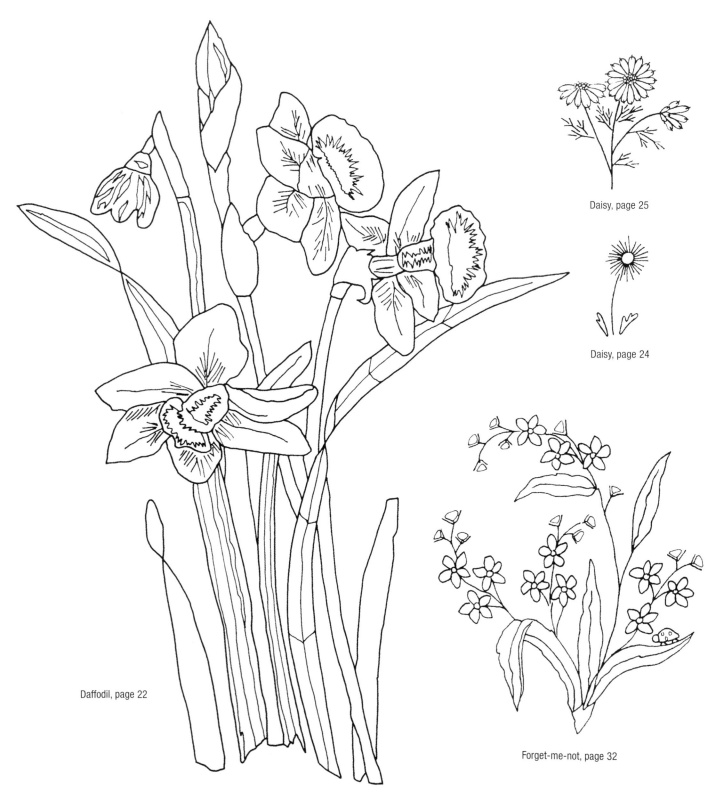

Daisy, page 25

Daisy, page 24

Daffodil, page 22

Forget-me-not, page 32

English daisy, page 28

Forget-me-not, page 29

Foxglove, page 34

Daisy, page 27

Daisies, page 26

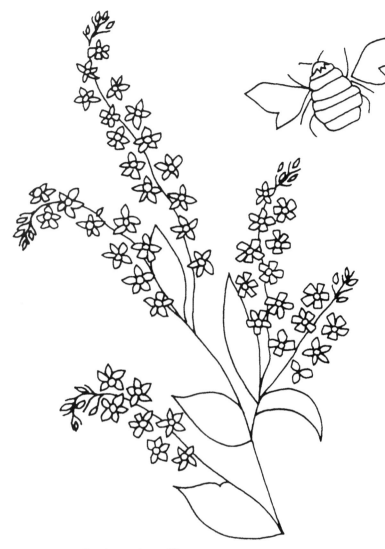

Forget-me-not, page 30

Forget-me-not, page 31

Forget-me-not, page 33

Frangipani, page 35

Fuchsia, page 36

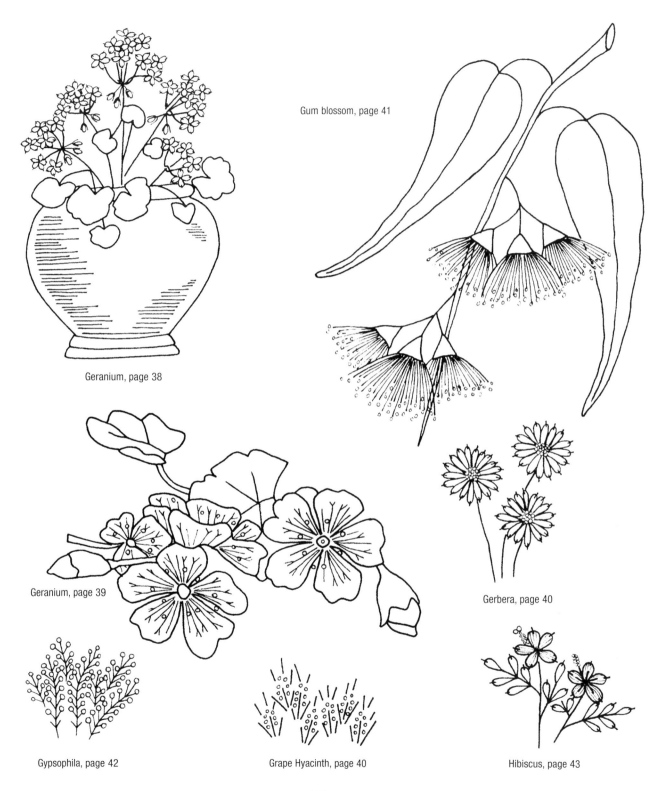

Geranium, page 38

Gum blossom, page 41

Geranium, page 39

Gerbera, page 40

Gypsophila, page 42

Grape Hyacinth, page 40

Hibiscus, page 43

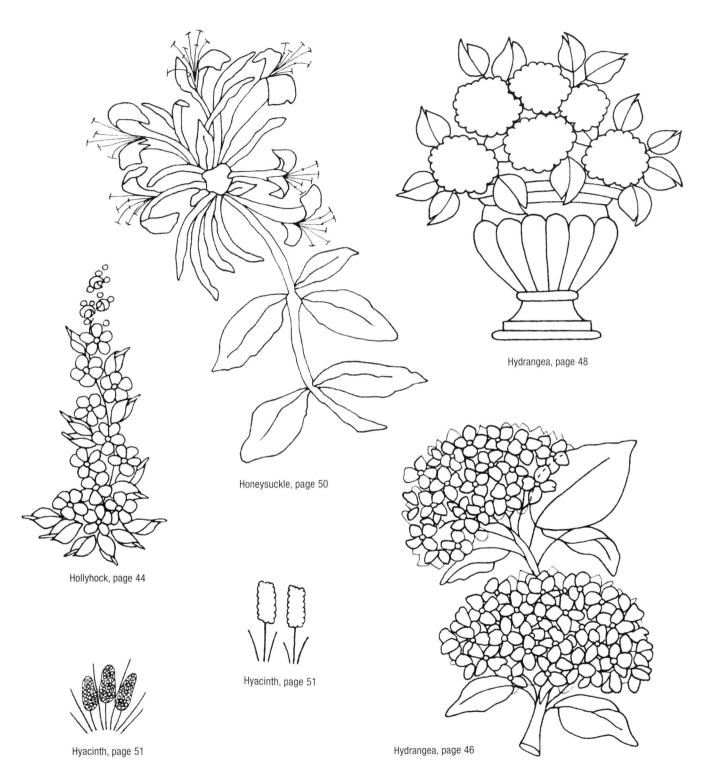

Honeysuckle, page 50

Hydrangea, page 48

Hollyhock, page 44

Hyacinth, page 51

Hyacinth, page 51

Hydrangea, page 46

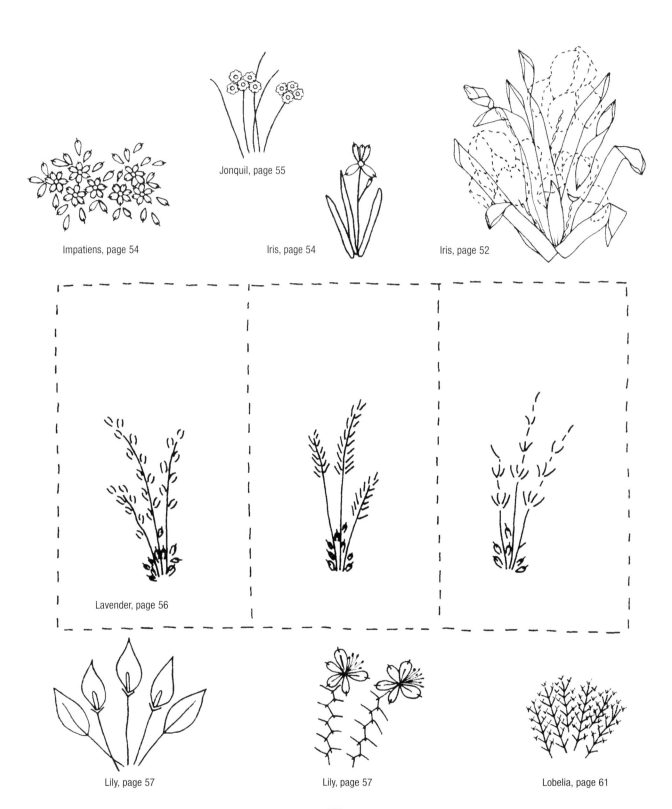

Impatiens, page 54

Jonquil, page 55

Iris, page 54

Iris, page 52

Lavender, page 56

Lily, page 57

Lily, page 57

Lobelia, page 61

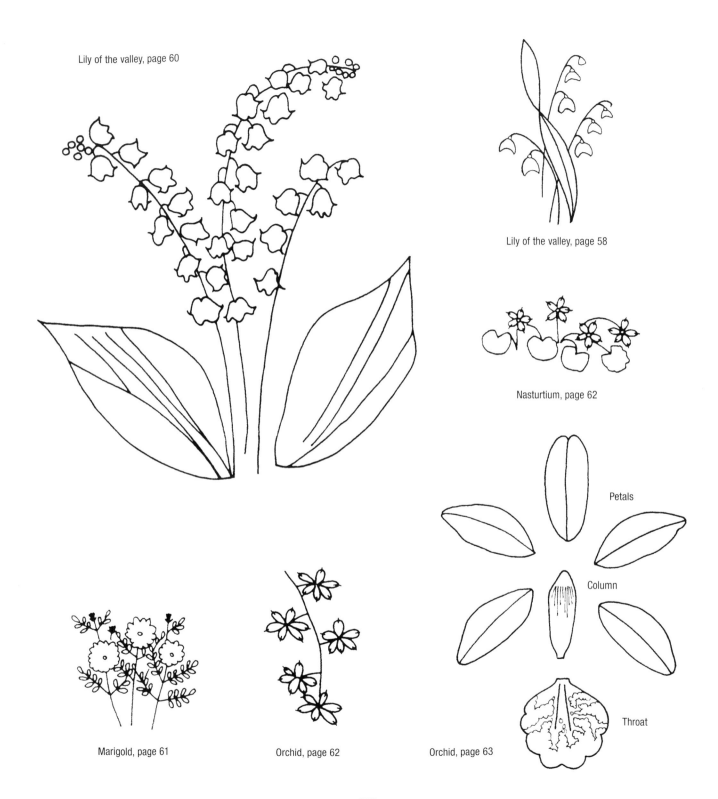

Lily of the valley, page 60

Lily of the valley, page 58

Nasturtium, page 62

Petals

Column

Throat

Marigold, page 61

Orchid, page 62

Orchid, page 63

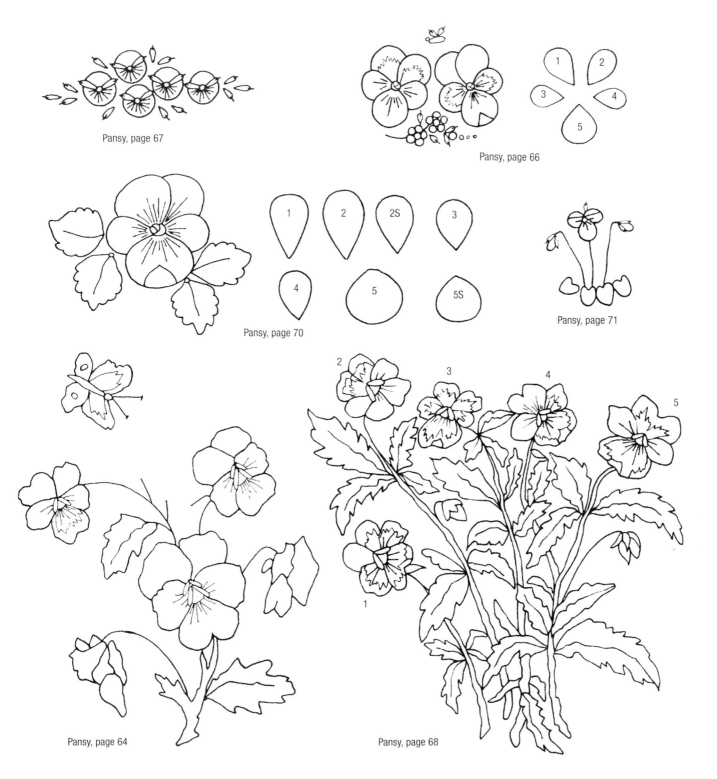

Pansy, page 67

Pansy, page 66

Pansy, page 70

Pansy, page 71

Pansy, page 64

Pansy, page 68

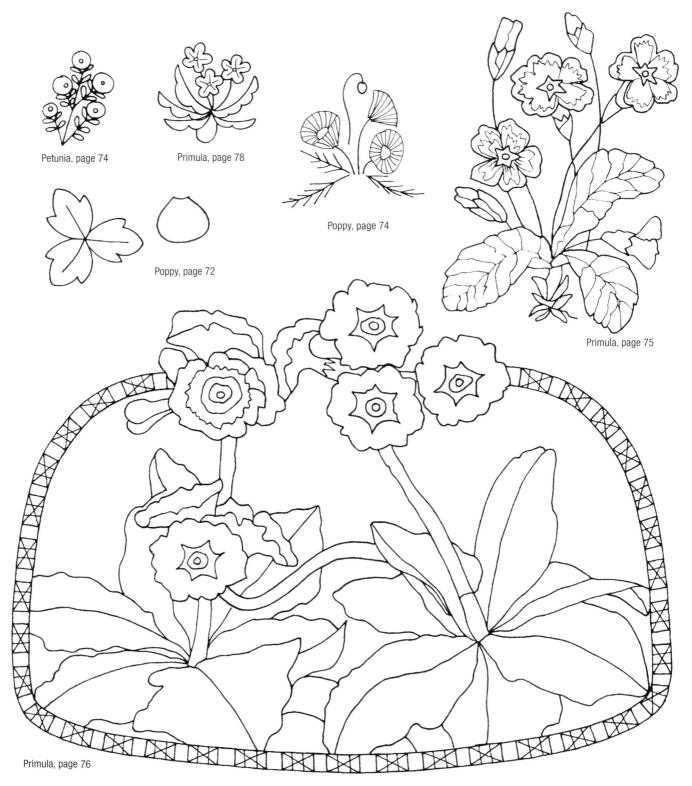

Petunia, page 74

Primula, page 78

Poppy, page 74

Poppy, page 72

Primula, page 75

Primula, page 76

Rose, page 85

Queen Anne's lace, page 79

Rose, page 86

Rose, page 84

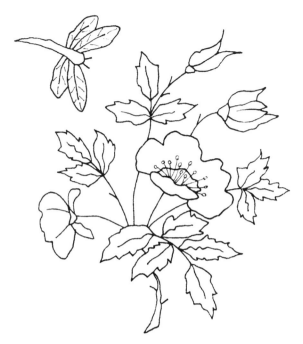

Rose, page 80

Salvia, page 91

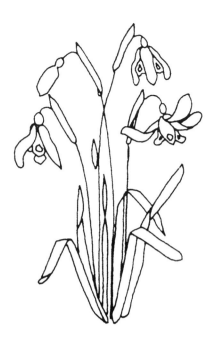

Snowdrop, page 88

Statice, page 91

Rose, page 82

Sunflower, page 92

Sunflower, page 93

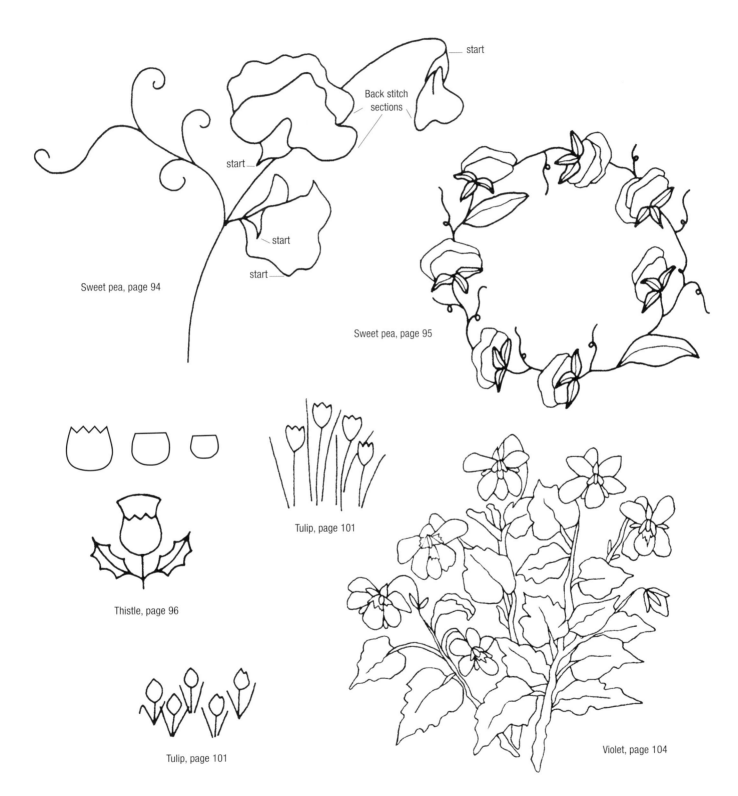

start

Back stitch
sections

start

start

Sweet pea, page 94

start

Sweet pea, page 95

Thistle, page 96

Tulip, page 101

Tulip, page 101

Violet, page 104

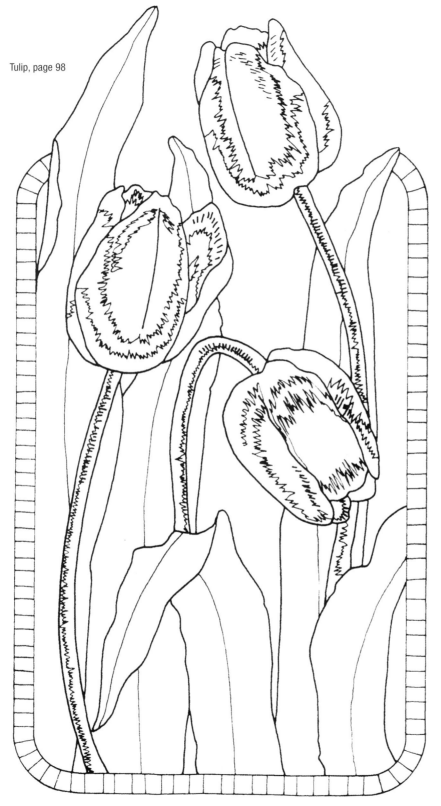

Tulip, page 98

Violet, page 106

Violet, page 102

Violet, page 105

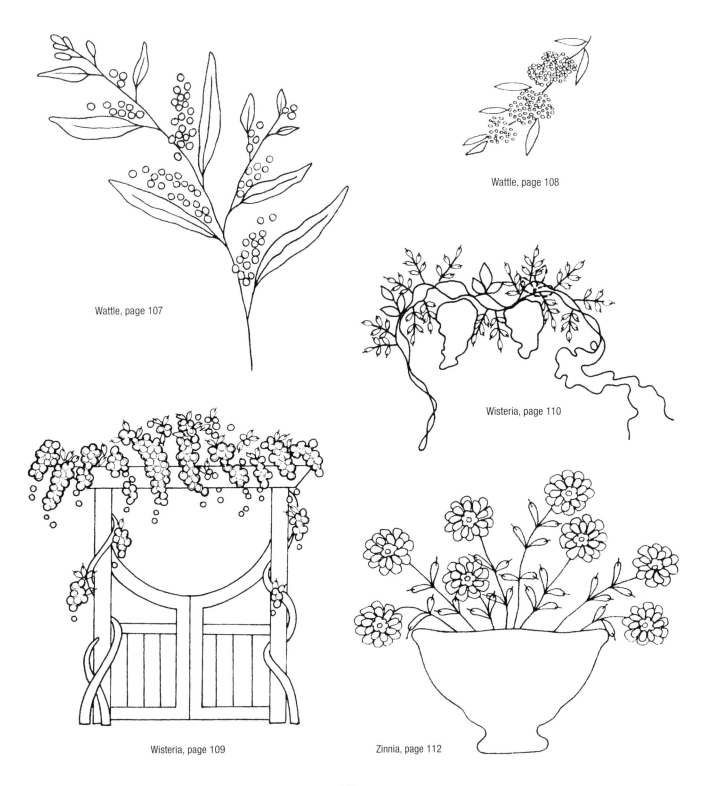

Wattle, page 107

Wattle, page 108

Wisteria, page 110

Wisteria, page 109

Zinnia, page 112

Index

First published in Great Britain 2016

Search Press Limited
Wellwood, North Farm Road,
Tunbridge Wells, Kent TN2 3DR

First published in Australia by
Country Bumpkin Publications
© Country Bumpkin Publications

ISBN: 978-1-78221-168-6

The Publishers and author can accept no
responsibility for any consequences arising
from the information, advice or instructions
given in this publication.

Suppliers
If you have difficulty in obtaining any of
the materials and equipment mentioned in
this book, then please visit the Search Press
website for details of suppliers:
www.searchpress.com

Printed in China